Python Natural Language Processing Cookbook

Over 50 recipes to understand, analyze, and generate text for implementing language processing tasks

Zhenya Antić

BIRMINGHAM—MUMBAI

Python Natural Language Processing Cookbook

Group Product Manager: Kunal Parikh
Publishing Product Manager: Aditi Gour
Senior Editor: Mohammed Yusuf Imaratwale
Content Development Editor: Nazia Shaikh
Technical Editor: Manikandan Kurup
Copy Editor: Safis Editing
Project Coordinator: Aishwarya Mohan
Proofreader: Safis Editing
Indexer: Priyanka Dhadke
Production Designer: Roshan Kawale

First published: March 2021
Production reference: 2220421

Published by Packt Publishing Ltd.
Livery Place
35 Livery Street
Birmingham
B3 2PB, UK.

ISBN 978-1-83898-731-2

www.packt.com

Contributors

About the author

Zhenya Antić is a **Natural Language Processing (NLP)** professional working at Practical Linguistics Inc. She helps businesses to improve processes and increase productivity by automating text processing. Zhenya holds a PhD in linguistics from University of California Berkeley and a BS in computer science from Massachusetts Institute of Technology.

I would like to thank those who helped this book come to life. The whole Packt team, including Ali Abidi, Gebin George, Nazia Shaikh, Aayan Hoda, Steffie Rodrigues and Pooja Yadav, has been really helpful, providing insight and tips when necessary.

I would also like to thank all the technical reviewers, including Mayank Rasu and Dylan Vivier, as well as Vera Gor, for their insightful comments about the code.

A special thanks goes to Miloš Babić, who reviewed the whole book, and Andjelka Zečević, who reviewed the deep learning sections. They provided very useful feedback.

Finally, I would like to thank my family for their constant support.

About the reviewers

Mayank Rasu is the author of the book *Hands-On Natural Language Processing with Python*. He has more than 12 years of global experience as a data scientist and quantitative analyst in the investment banking domain. He has worked at the intersection of finance and technology and has developed and deployed AI-based applications in the finance domain, which include sentiment analyzer, robotics process automation, and deep learning-based document reviewers. Mayank is also an educator and has trained/mentored working professionals on applied AI.

Dylan Vivier is a data science enthusiast with experience in the automotive, oil and gas, and shipbuilding industries. With engineering degrees from both the University of Detroit and Purdue University, he has also studied at the Indiana University Luddy School of Informatics, Computing, and Engineering. In his spare time, Dylan enjoys researching new applications for data science and playing chess. Diversity and inclusion, Agile project development, Python, SQL, algorithms, data structures, **Condition-based Maintenance (CBM)**, cybersecurity, machine learning, **Natural Language Processing (NLP)**, **Internet of Things (IoT)**, AI, and Blockchain are some of his other interests.

Table of Contents

Preface

1

Learning NLP Basics

2
Playing with Grammar

3
Representing Text – Capturing Semantics

4

Classifying Texts

7

Building Chatbots

8

Visualizing Text Data

Other Books You May Enjoy

Index

Preface

Python is the most widely used language for natural language processing (NLP) thanks to its extensive tools and libraries for analyzing text and extracting computer-usable data. This book will take you through a range of techniques for text processing, from basics such as parsing parts of speech to complex topics such as topic modeling, text classification, and visualization.

Starting with an overview of NLP, the book presents recipes for dividing text into sentences, stemming and lemmatization, removing stopwords, and parts-of-speech tagging to help you to prepare your data. You'll then learn about ways of extracting and representing grammatical information, such as dependency parsing and anaphora resolution, discover different ways of representing the semantics using bag of words, TF-IDF, word embeddings, and BERT, and develop skills for text classification using keywords, SVMs, LSTMs, and other techniques. As you advance, you'll also see how to extract information from text, implement unsupervised and supervised techniques for topic modeling, and perform topic modeling of short texts, such as tweets. Additionally, the book covers developing chatbots using NLTK and Rasa, and visualizing text data.

By the end of this NLP book, you'll have developed the skills to use a powerful set of tools for text processing.

Who this book is for

This book is for data scientists and professionals who want to learn how to work with text. Intermediate knowledge of Python will help you to make the most out of this book. If you are an NLP practitioner, this book will serve as a code reference when working on your projects.

What this book covers

Chapter 1, Learning NLP Basics, is an introductory chapter with basic preprocessing steps for working with text. It includes recipes such as dividing up text into sentences, stemming and lemmatization, removing stopwords, and parts-of-speech tagging. You will find out about different approaches for parts-of-speech tagging, as well as two options for removing stopwords.

Chapter 2, Playing with Grammar, will show how to get and use grammatical information about text. We will create a dependency parse and then use it to split a sentence into clauses. We will also use the dependency parse and noun chunks to extract entities and relations in the text. Certain recipes will show how to extract grammatical information in both English and Spanish.

Chapter 3, Representing Text – Capturing Semantics, covers how, as working with words and semantics is easy for people but difficult for computers, we need to represent text in a way other than words in order for computers to be able to work with the text. This chapter presents different ways of representing text, from a simple bag of words, to BERT. This chapter also discusses a basic implementation of semantic search that uses these semantic representations.

Chapter 4, Classifying Texts, covers text classification, which is one of the most important techniques in NLP. It is used in many different industries for different types of texts, such as tweets, long documents, and sentences. In this chapter, you will learn how to do both supervised and unsupervised text classification with a variety of techniques and tools, including K-Means, SVMs and LSTMs.

Chapter 5, Getting Started with Information Extraction, discusses how one of the main goals of NLP is extracting information from text in order to use it later. This chapter shows different ways of pulling information from text, from the simplest regular expression techniques to find emails and URLs to neural network tools to extract sentiment.

Chapter 6, Topic Modeling, discusses how determining topics of texts is an important NLP tool that can help in text classification and discovering new topics in texts. This chapter introduces different techniques for topic modeling, including unsupervised and supervised techniques, and topic modeling of short texts, such as tweets.

Chapter 7, Building Chatbots, covers chatbots, which are an important marketing tool that has emerged in the last few years. In this chapter, you will learn how to build a chatbot using two different frameworks, NLTK for keyword matching chatbots, and Rasa for sophisticated chatbots with a deep learning model under the hood.

Chapter 8, Visualizing Text Data, discusses how visualizing the results of different NLP analyses can be a very useful tool for presentation and evaluation. This chapter introduces you to visualization techniques for different NLP tools, including NER, topic modeling, and word clouds.

To get the most out of this book

You will need Python 3 installed on your system. We recommend installing the Python libraries discussed in this book using `pip`. The code snippets in the book mention the relevant command to install a given library on the Windows OS.

Software/hardware covered in the book	OS requirements
Python 3.x, Anaconda, Jupyter Notebook	Windows/macOS/Linux

If you are using the digital version of this book, we advise you to type the code yourself or access the code via the GitHub repository (link available in the next section). Doing so will help you avoid any potential errors related to the copying and pasting of code.

Download the example code files

You can download the example code files for this book from GitHub at `https://github.com/PacktPublishing/Python-Natural-Language-Processing-Cookbook`. In case there's an update to the code, it will be updated on the existing GitHub repository.

We also have other code bundles from our rich catalog of books and videos available at `https://github.com/PacktPublishing/`. Check them out!

Download the color images

We also provide a PDF file that has color images of the screenshots/diagrams used in this book. You can download it here: `https://static.packt-cdn.com/downloads/9781838987312_ColorImages.pdf`.

Conventions used

There are a number of text conventions used throughout this book.

`Code in text`: Indicates code words in text, database table names, folder names, filenames, file extensions, pathnames, dummy URLs, user input, and Twitter handles. Here is an example: "For this recipe, we will need just the beginning of the book, which can be found in the `sherlock_holmes_1.txt` file."

A block of code is set as follows:

```
filename = "sherlock_holmes_1.txt"
file = open(filename, "r", encoding="utf-8")
text = file.read()
```

When we wish to draw your attention to a particular part of a code block, the relevant lines or items are set in bold:

```
import time
start = time.time()
main()
print("%s s" % (time.time() - start))
```

Any command-line input or output is written as follows:

```
python -m spacy download es_core_news_sm
```

Bold: Indicates a new term, an important word, or words that you see onscreen. For example, words in menus or dialog boxes appear in the text like this. Here is an example: "It shows that three words from the vocabulary are present, which are **seen**, **of**, and **Holmes**."

> **Tips or important notes**
> Appear like this.

Sections

In this book, you will find several headings that appear frequently (*Getting ready*, *How to do it...*, *How it works...*, *There's more...*, and *See also*).

To give clear instructions on how to complete a recipe, use these sections as follows:

Getting ready

This section tells you what to expect in the recipe and describes how to set up any software or any preliminary settings required for the recipe.

How to do it...

This section contains the steps required to follow the recipe.

How it works...

This section usually consists of a detailed explanation of what happened in the previous section.

There's more...

This section consists of additional information about the recipe in order to make you more knowledgeable about the recipe.

See also

This section provides helpful links to other useful information for the recipe.

Get in touch

Feedback from our readers is always welcome.

General feedback: If you have questions about any aspect of this book, mention the book title in the subject of your message and email us at customercare@packtpub.com.

Errata: Although we have taken every care to ensure the accuracy of our content, mistakes do happen. If you have found a mistake in this book, we would be grateful if you would report this to us. Please visit www.packtpub.com/support/errata, selecting your book, clicking on the Errata Submission Form link, and entering the details.

Piracy: If you come across any illegal copies of our works in any form on the Internet, we would be grateful if you would provide us with the location address or website name. Please contact us at copyright@packt.com with a link to the material.

If you are interested in becoming an author: If there is a topic that you have expertise in and you are interested in either writing or contributing to a book, please visit authors. packtpub.com.

Reviews

Please leave a review. Once you have read and used this book, why not leave a review on the site that you purchased it from? Potential readers can then see and use your unbiased opinion to make purchase decisions, we at Packt can understand what you think about our products, and our authors can see your feedback on their book. Thank you!

For more information about Packt, please visit packt.com.

1
Learning NLP Basics

While working on this book, I focused on including recipes that would be useful in a wide variety of **NLP** (**Natural Language Processing**) projects. They range from the simple to the advanced, and deal with everything from grammar to visualizations; and in many of them, options for languages other than English are included. I hope you find the book useful.

Before we can get on with the real work of NLP, we need to prepare our text for processing. This chapter will show you how to do that. By the end of the chapter, you will be able to have a list of words in a piece of text arranged with their parts of speech and lemmas or stems, and with very frequent words removed.

NLTK and **spaCy** are two important packages that we will be working with in this chapter and throughout the book.

The recipes included in this chapter are as follows:

- Dividing text into sentences
- Dividing sentences into words: tokenization
- Parts of speech tagging
- Stemming
- Combining similar words: lemmatization
- Removing stopwords

Technical requirements

Throughout this book, I will be showing examples that were run using an **Anaconda** installation of **Python 3.6.10**. To install Anaconda, follow the instructions here: https://docs.anaconda.com/anaconda/install/.

After you have installed Anaconda, use it to create a virtual environment:

```
conda create -n nlp_book python=3.6.10 anaconda
activate nlp_book
```

Then, install spaCy 2.3.0 and NLTK 3.4.5:

```
pip install nltk
pip install spacy
```

After you have installed spaCy and NLTK, install the models needed to use them. For spaCy, use this:

```
python -m spacy download en_core_web_sm
```

Use Python commands to download the necessary model for NLTK:

```
python
>>> import nltk
>>> nltk.download('punkt')
```

All the code that is in this book can be found in the book's GitHub repository: https://github.com/PacktPublishing/Python-Natural-Language-Processing-Cookbook.

> **Important note**
> The files in the book's GitHub repository should be run using the -m option from the main directory that contains the code subfolders for each chapter. For example, you would use it as follows:

```
python -m Chapter01.dividing_into_sentences
```

Dividing text into sentences

When we work with text, we can work with text units on different scales: we can work at the level of the document itself, such as a newspaper article; the paragraph, the sentence, or the word. Sentences are the main unit of processing in many NLP tasks. In this section, I will show you how to divide text into sentences.

Getting ready

For this part, we will be using the text of the book *The Adventures of Sherlock Holmes*. You can find the whole text in the book's GitHub (see the `sherlock_holmes.txt` file). For this recipe, we will need just the beginning of the book, which can be found in the `sherlock_holmes_1.txt` file.

In order to do this task, you will need the `nltk` package and its sentence tokenizers, described in the *Technical requirements* section.

How to do it...

We will now divide the text of *The Adventures of Sherlock Holmes*, outputting a list of sentences:

1. Import the `nltk` package:

    ```
    import nltk
    ```

2. Read in the book text:

    ```
    filename = "sherlock_holmes_1.txt"
    file = open(filename, "r", encoding="utf-8")
    text = file.read()
    ```

3. Replace newlines with spaces:

    ```
    text = text.replace("\n", " ")
    ```

4. Initialize an NLTK tokenizer. This uses the `punkt` model we downloaded previously:

    ```
    tokenizer = nltk.data.load("tokenizers/punkt/english.
    pickle")
    ```

5. Divide the text into sentences:

```
sentences = tokenizer.tokenize(text)
```

The resulting list, sentences, has all the sentences in the first part of the book:

```
['To Sherlock Holmes she is always _the_ woman.', 'I have
seldom heard him mention her under any other name.',
'In his eyes she eclipses and predominates the whole of
her sex.', 'It was not that he felt any emotion akin
to love for Irene Adler.', 'All emotions, and that one
particularly, were abhorrent to his cold, precise but
admirably balanced mind.', 'He was, I take it, the most
perfect reasoning and observing machine that the world
has seen, but as a lover he would have placed himself
in a false position.', 'He never spoke of the softer
passions, save with a gibe and a sneer.', 'They were
admirable things for the observer—excellent for drawing
the veil from men's motives and actions.', 'But for the
trained reasoner to admit such intrusions into his own
delicate and finely adjusted temperament was to introduce
a distracting factor which might throw a doubt upon all
his mental results.', 'Grit in a sensitive instrument,
or a crack in one of his own high-power lenses, would
not be more disturbing than a strong emotion in a nature
such as his.', 'And yet there was but one woman to him,
and that woman was the late Irene Adler, of dubious and
questionable memory.']
```

How it works...

In *step 1*, we import the nltk package. In *step 2*, we open the text file and read the contents into a string. In *step 3*, we replace newlines with spaces. This is an optional step, and I include it for better readability. In *step 4*, we initialize the NLTK tokenizer. In *step 5*, we use the tokenizer to divide the text into sentences.

Although it might seem straightforward to instead just divide text into sentences by just using a regular expression to split at the periods, in reality, it is more complicated. We use periods in places other than ends of sentences, for example, after abbreviations. Similarly, while all sentences in English start with a capital letter, we also use capital letters for proper names.

There's more...

We can also use a different strategy to parse the text into sentences, employing another very popular NLP package, spaCy. Here is how it works:

1. Import the `spacy` package:

    ```
    import spacy
    ```

2. Read in the book text:

    ```
    filename = "sherlock_holmes_1.txt"
    file = open(filename, "r", encoding="utf-8")
    text = file.read()
    ```

3. Replace newlines with spaces:

    ```
    text = text.replace("\n", " ")
    ```

4. Initialize the spaCy engine:

    ```
    nlp = spacy.load("en_core_web_sm")
    ```

5. Divide the text into sentences:

    ```
    doc = nlp(text)
    sentences = [sentence.text for sentence in doc.sents]
    ```

    The result will be the sentences in the first part of *The Adventures of Sherlock Holmes*:

    ```
    ['To Sherlock Holmes she is always _the_ woman.', 'I have
    seldom heard him mention her under any other name.',
    'In his eyes she eclipses and predominates the whole of
    her sex.', 'It was not that he felt any emotion akin
    to love for Irene Adler.', 'All emotions, and that one
    particularly, were abhorrent to his cold, precise but
    admirably balanced mind.', 'He was, I take it, the most
    perfect reasoning and observing machine that the world
    has seen, but as a lover he would have placed himself
    in a false position.', 'He never spoke of the softer
    passions, save with a gibe and a sneer.', 'They were
    admirable things for the observer—excellent for drawing
    the veil from men's motives and actions.', 'But for the
    trained reasoner to admit such intrusions into his own
    delicate and finely adjusted temperament was to introduce
    ```

```
a distracting factor which might throw a doubt upon all
his mental results.', 'Grit in a sensitive instrument,
or a crack in one of his own high-power lenses, would
not be more disturbing than a strong emotion in a nature
such as his.', 'And yet there was but one woman to him,
and that woman was the late Irene Adler, of dubious and
questionable memory.']
```

An important difference between spaCy and NLTK is the time it takes to complete the sentence-splitting process. We can time the execution by using the `time` package and putting the code to split the sentences into the `main` function:

```
import time
start = time.time()
main()
print("%s s" % (time.time() - start))
```

The spaCy algorithm takes 0.062 seconds, while the NLTK algorithm takes 0.004 seconds. It is possible that you will get slightly different values. Make sure that the time you measure is not that of the first run, as it is always the slowest one.

The reason why you might use spaCy is if you are doing other processing with the package along with splitting it into sentences. The spaCy processor does many other things, and that is why it takes longer. If you are using other features of spaCy, there is no reason to use NLTK just for sentence splitting, and it's better to employ spaCy for the whole pipeline.

It is also possible to use just the tokenizer from spaCy; please see their documentation for more information: https://spacy.io/usage/processing-pipelines.

> **Important note**
> spaCy might be slower, but it does many more things in the background; if you are using its other features, use it for sentence splitting as well.

See also

You can use NLTK and spaCy to divide text in languages other than English. NLTK includes tokenizer models for Czech, Danish, Dutch, Estonian, Finnish, French, German, Greek, Italian, Norwegian, Polish, Portuguese, Slovene, Spanish, Swedish, and Turkish. In order to load those models, use the name of the language followed by the `.pickle` extension:

```
tokenizer = nltk.data.load("tokenizers/punkt/spanish.pickle")
```

See the NLTK documentation to find out more: `https://www.nltk.org/index.html`.

Likewise, spaCy has models for other languages: Chinese, Danish, Dutch, English, French, German, Greek, Italian, Japanese, Lithuanian, Norwegian, Polish, Portuguese, Romanian, and Spanish. In order to use those models, you would have to download them separately. For example, for Spanish, use this command to download the model:

```
python -m spacy download es_core_news_sm
```

And then put this line in the code to use it:

```
nlp = spacy.load("es_core_news_sm")
```

See the spaCy documentation to find out more: `https://spacy.io/usage/models`.

Dividing sentences into words – tokenization

In many instances, we rely on individual words when we do NLP tasks. This happens, for example, when we build semantic models of texts by relying on the semantics of individual words, or when we are looking for words with a specific part of speech. To divide text into words, we can use NLTK and spaCy.

Getting ready

For this recipe, we will be using the same text of the book *The Adventures of Sherlock Holmes*. You can find the whole text in the book's GitHub repository. For this recipe, we will need just the beginning of the book, which can be found in the `sherlock_holmes_1.txt` file.

In order to do this task, you will need the `nltk` package, described in the *Technical requirements* section.

How to do it...

1. Import the `nltk` package:

    ```
    import nltk
    ```

2. Read in the book text:

    ```
    filename = "sherlock_holmes_1.txt"
    file = open(filename, "r", encoding="utf-8")
    text = file.read()
    ```

3. Replace newlines with spaces:

    ```
    text = text.replace("\n", " ")
    ```

4. Divide the text into words:

    ```
    words = nltk.tokenize.word_tokenize(text)
    ```

    The output will be the list of words in the text:

    ```
    ['To', 'Sherlock', 'Holmes', 'she', 'is', 'always', '_
    the_', 'woman', '.', 'I', 'have', 'seldom', 'heard',
    'him', 'mention', 'her', 'under', 'any', 'other',
    'name', '.', 'In', 'his', 'eyes', 'she', 'eclipses',
    'and', 'predominates', 'the', 'whole', 'of', 'her',
    'sex', '.', 'It', 'was', 'not', 'that', 'he', 'felt',
    'any', 'emotion', 'akin', 'to', 'love', 'for', 'Irene',
    'Adler', '.', 'All', 'emotions', ',', 'and', 'that',
    'one', 'particularly', ',', 'were', 'abhorrent', 'to',
    'his', 'cold', ',', 'precise', 'but', 'admirably',
    'balanced', 'mind', '.', 'He', 'was', ',', 'I', 'take',
    'it', ',', 'the', 'most', 'perfect', 'reasoning',
    'and', 'observing', 'machine', 'that', 'the', 'world',
    'has', 'seen', ',', 'but', 'as', 'a', 'lover', 'he',
    'would', 'have', 'placed', 'himself', 'in', 'a', 'false',
    'position', '.', 'He', 'never', 'spoke', 'of', 'the',
    'softer', 'passions', ',', 'save', 'with', 'a', 'gibe',
    'and', 'a', 'sneer', '.', 'They', 'were', 'admirable',
    'things', 'for', 'the', 'observer—excellent', 'for',
    'drawing', 'the', 'veil', 'from', 'men', ''', 's',
    'motives', 'and', 'actions', '.', 'But', 'for',
    'the', 'trained', 'reasoner', 'to', 'admit', 'such',
    'intrusions', 'into', 'his', 'own', 'delicate', 'and',
    'finely', 'adjusted', 'temperament', 'was', 'to',
    ```

```
'introduce', 'a', 'distracting', 'factor', 'which',
'might', 'throw', 'a', 'doubt', 'upon', 'all', 'his',
'mental', 'results', '.', 'Grit', 'in', 'a', 'sensitive',
'instrument', ',', 'or', 'a', 'crack', 'in', 'one', 'of',
'his', 'own', 'high-power', 'lenses', ',', 'would',
'not', 'be', 'more', 'disturbing', 'than', 'a', 'strong',
'emotion', 'in', 'a', 'nature', 'such', 'as', 'his',
'.', 'And', 'yet', 'there', 'was', 'but', 'one', 'woman',
'to', 'him', ',', 'and', 'that', 'woman', 'was', 'the',
'late', 'Irene', 'Adler', ',', 'of', 'dubious', 'and',
'questionable', 'memory', '.']
```

How it works...

In *step 1*, we import the `nltk` package. In *step 2*, we open the text file and read its contents into a string. *Step 3* is optional: we replace newlines with spaces for readability.

In *step 4*, we divide the text into words using the `nltk.tokenize.word_tokenize()` function. The output is a list, where each token is either a word or a punctuation mark. The NLTK tokenizer uses a set of rules to split the text into words. It splits but does not expand contractions, such as *don't → do n't and men's → men 's*, as in the preceding example. It treats punctuation and quotes as separate tokens, so the result includes words with no other marks.

There's more...

NLTK has a special tokenizer for tweets and similar short texts. It has the options of removing Twitter user handles and shortening repeating characters to a maximum of three in a row. For example, let's use a made-up tweet: *@EmpireStateBldg Central Park Tower is reaaaaally hiiiiiiigh* and tokenize it with NLTK Twitter tokenizer:

1. Import the `nltk` package:

    ```
    import nltk
    ```

2. Initialize the `tweet` variable:

    ```
    tweet = "@EmpireStateBldg Central Park Tower is reaaaally
    hiiiigh"
    ```

3. Divide the text into words. Set the parameters to preserve case, reduce the length, and strip the handles:

```
words = \
nltk.tokenize.casual.casual_tokenize(tweet,
                              preserve_case=True,
                              reduce_len=True,
                              strip_handles=True)
```

The output will be a list of words:

```
['Central', 'Park', 'Tower', 'is', 'reaaally', 'hiiigh']
```

The repetition of characters in the words *reaaaaally* and *hiiiiiiigh* is shortened to three, the twitter handle *@EmpireStateBldg* has been removed, and the words have been tokenized.

We can also use spaCy to do the tokenization. Word tokenization is one task in a larger array of tasks that spaCy accomplishes while processing text. Here is how it works:

4. Import the `spacy` package:

```
import spacy
```

5. Read in the book text:

```
filename = "sherlock_holmes_1.txt"
file = open(filename, "r", encoding="utf-8")
text = file.read()
```

6. Replace newlines with spaces:

```
text = text.replace("\n", " ")
```

7. Initialize the spaCy engine using the English model:

```
nlp = spacy.load("en_core_web_sm")
```

8. Divide the text into sentences:

```
doc = nlp(text)
words = [token.text for token in doc]
```

> **Important note**
> If you are doing other processing with spaCy, it makes sense to use it.
> Otherwise, NLTK word tokenization is sufficient.

See also

The NLTK package only has word tokenization for English.

spaCy has models for several other languages: Chinese, Danish, Dutch, English, French, German, Greek, Italian, Japanese, Lithuanian, Norwegian, Polish, Portuguese, Romanian, and Spanish. In order to use those models, you would have to download them separately. For example, for Spanish, use this command to download the model:

```
python -m spacy download es_core_news_sm
```

And then put this line in the code to use it:

```
nlp = spacy.load("es_core_news_sm")
```

See the spaCy documentation to find out more: `https://spacy.io/usage/models`.

Parts of speech tagging

In many cases, NLP processing depends on determining the parts of speech of the words in the text. For example, in sentence classification, we sometimes use the parts of speech of the words as a feature that is input to the classifier. In this recipe, we will again consider the NLTK and spaCy algorithms.

Getting ready

For this recipe, we will be using the same text of the book *The Adventures of Sherlock Holmes*. You can find the whole text in the book's GitHub. For this recipe, we will need just the beginning of the book, which can be found in the `sherlock_holmes_1.txt` file.

In order to do this task, you will need the spaCy package, described in the *Technical requirements* section.

How to do it...

In this recipe, we will use the spaCy package to label words with their parts of speech, and I will show that it is superior to NLTK in this task.

The process is as follows:

1. Import the spacy package:

```
import spacy
```

2. Read in the book text:

```
filename = "sherlock_holmes_1.txt"
file = open(filename, "r", encoding="utf-8")
text = file.read()
```

3. Replace newlines with spaces:

```
text = text.replace("\n", " ")
```

4. Initialize the spaCy engine:

```
nlp = spacy.load("en_core_web_sm")
```

5. Use the spaCy engine to process the text:

```
doc = nlp(text)
```

6. Get the list of tuples with words and parts of speech tags:

```
words = [token.text for token in doc]
pos = [token.pos_ for token in doc]
word_pos_tuples = list(zip(words, pos))
```

Part of the result is shown here; for the rest, please see the book's GitHub:

```
[('To', 'ADP'), ('Sherlock', 'PROPN'), ('Holmes',
'PROPN'), ('she', 'PRON'), ('is', 'VERB'), ('always',
'ADV'), ('_', 'NOUN'), ('the', 'DET'), ('_', 'NOUN'),
('woman', 'NOUN'), ('.', 'PUNCT'), …]
```

The resulting list contains tuples of words and parts of speech. The list of parts of speech tags is available here: https://universaldependencies.org/docs/u/pos/.

How it works...

In *step 1*, we import the spacy package. In *step 2*, we read in the text file. In the optional *step 3*, we replace newlines with spaces.

In *step 4*, we initialize the spaCy engine, and in *step 5*, we use it to process the text. The resulting `Document` object contains an iterator with `Token` objects, and each `Token` object has the information about parts of speech.

In *step 6*, we create two lists, one with words and one with their corresponding parts of speech, and then combine them into a list of tuples. We do this in order to easily print the whole list with their corresponding parts of speech. When you use parts of speech tagging in your code, you can just iterate through the list of tokens. The result shows the final list of word-parts of speech tuples.

There's more...

We can compare spaCy's performance to NLTK in this task. Here are the steps for getting the parts of speech with NLTK:

1. Import the `nltk` package:

    ```
    import nltk
    ```

2. Read in the book text:

    ```
    filename = "sherlock_holmes_1.txt"
    file = open(filename, "r", encoding="utf-8")
    text = file.read()
    ```

3. Replace newlines with spaces:

    ```
    text = text.replace("\n", " ")
    ```

4. Tokenize the text into `words`:

    ```
    words = nltk.tokenize.word_tokenize(text)
    ```

5. Process the list of words with the NLTK parts of speech tagger:

    ```
    words_with_pos = nltk.pos_tag(words)
    ```

6. This is the partial result. For the whole output please see the book's GitHub:

    ```
    [('To', 'TO'), ('Sherlock', 'NNP'), ('Holmes', 'NNP'),
    ('she', 'PRP'), ('is', 'VBZ'), ('always', 'RB'), ('_
    the_', 'JJ'), ('woman', 'NN'), ('.', '.'), …]
    ```

The list of part of speech tags that NLTK uses is different from spaCy:

```python
>>> import nltk
>>> nltk.download('tagsets')
>>> nltk.help.upenn_tagset()
```

Comparing the performance, we see that spaCy takes 0.065 seconds, while NLTK takes 0.170 seconds, so spaCy is more efficient. Also, the parts of speech information is already available in the spaCy objects after the initial processing has been done.

> **Important note**
>
> spaCy does all of its processing at once, and the results are stored in the Doc object. The parts of speech information is available by iterating through Token objects.

See also

If you would like to tag text that's in another language, you can do so by using spaCy's models for other languages. For example, we can load the Spanish spaCy model to run it on Spanish text:

```
nlp = spacy.load("es_core_news_sm")
```

If spaCy doesn't have a model for the language you are working with, you can train your own model with spaCy. See https://spacy.io/usage/training#tagger-parser.

Word stemming

In some NLP tasks, we need to **stem** words, or remove the suffixes and endings such as -*ing* and -*ed*. This recipe shows how to do that.

Getting ready

To do this recipe, we will be using NLTK and its **Snowball Stemmer**.

How to do it...

We will load the NLTK Snowball Stemmer and use it to stem words:

1. Import the NLTK Snowball Stemmer:

    ```
    from nltk.stem.snowball import SnowballStemmer
    ```

2. Initialize `stemmer` with English:

    ```
    stemmer = SnowballStemmer('english')
    ```

3. Initialize a list with words to stem:

    ```
    words = ['leaf', 'leaves', 'booking', 'writing',
             'completed', 'stemming', 'skies']
    ```

4. Stem the words:

    ```
    stemmed_words = [stemmer.stem(word) for word in words]
    ```

    The result will be as follows:

    ```
    ['leaf', 'leav', 'book', 'write', 'complet', 'stem',
    'sky']
    ```

How it works...

In *step 1*, we import the `SnowballStemmer` object. In *step 2*, we initialize the `stemmer` object with English as the input language. In *step 3*, we create a list with words we would like to stem. In *step 4*, we create a list with the stemmed words.

The stemmer strips suffixes and endings from the words. As seen here, it removes suffixes such as *-es, -ing,* and *-ed*, as well as others, such as *-ive, -ize,* and *-ment*. It also handles exceptions, as seen in the case of *skies → sky*. However, it does not change the stem to its canonical form, as the example with the word *leaves* shows.

There's more...

The NLTK Snowball Stemmer has algorithms for several languages. To see all the languages the NLTK Snowball Stemmer uses, use this command:

```
print(SnowballStemmer.languages)
```

The result is as follows:

```
('danish', 'dutch', 'english', 'finnish', 'french', 'german',
'hungarian', 'italian', 'norwegian', 'porter', 'portuguese',
'romanian', 'russian', 'spanish', 'swedish')
```

For example, say we used it to stem these Spanish words:

```
stemmer = SnowballStemmer('spanish')
spanish_words = ['caminando', 'amigo', 'bueno']
stemmed_words = [stemmer.stem(word) for word in spanish_words]
```

The result would be as follows:

```
['camin', 'amig', 'buen']
```

See also

See `http://snowball.tartarus.org/algorithms/english/stemmer.html` for more information about the NLTK Snowball Stemmer.

Combining similar words – lemmatization

A similar technique to stemming is **lemmatization**. The difference is that lemmatization provides us with a real word, that is, its canonical form. For example, the lemma of the word *cats* is *cat*, and the lemma for the word *ran* is *run*.

Getting ready

We will be using the NLTK package for this recipe.

How to do it...

The NLTK package includes a `lemmatizer` module based on the WordNet database.

Here is how to use it:

1. Import the NLTK WordNet `lemmatizer`:

    ```
    from nltk.stem import WordNetLemmatizer
    ```

2. Initialize `lemmatizer`:

    ```
    lemmatizer = WordNetLemmatizer()
    ```

3. Initialize a list with words to lemmatize:

```
words = ['duck', 'geese', 'cats', 'books']
```

4. Lemmatize the words:

```
lemmatized_words = [lemmatizer.lemmatize(word) for word
in words]
```

5. The result will be as follows:

```
['duck', 'goose', 'cat', 'book']
```

How it works...

In *step 1*, we import `WordNetLemmatizer`, and in *step 2*, we initialize it. In *step 3*, we initialize a list of words we want to lemmatize. In *step 4*, we create a list with the lemmatized words. The result shows correct lemmatization for all words, including exceptions such as *geese*.

There's more...

The `lemmatize` function has a parameter, `pos` (for parts of speech), which is set to noun by default. If you would like to lemmatize a verb or an adjective, you have to explicitly specify it:

```
>>> lemmatizer.lemmatize('loved', 'v')
'love'
>>> lemmatizer.lemmatize('worse', 'a')
'bad'
```

There is no easy way to lemmatize adverbs.

We can combine parts of speech tagging and lemmatization:

1. Import helper functions from the `pos_tagging` module:

```
from Chapter01.pos_tagging import pos_tag_nltk, read_
text_file
```

2. Add a dictionary mapping from NLTK parts of speech tags to `lemmatizer`-accepted parts of speech tags and a separate set of tags accepted by `lemmatizer`:

```
pos_mapping = {'JJ':'a', 'JJR':'a', 'JJS':'a', 'NN':'n',
```

```
                    'NNS':'n', 'VBD':'v', 'VBG':'v',
                    'VBN':'v', 'VBP':'v', 'VBZ':'v'}
accepted_pos = {'a', 'v', 'n'}
```

3. Define the `lemmatize_long_text` function, which will take a long text, tag it with parts of speech, and then lemmatize adjectives, verbs, and nouns:

```
def lemmatize_long_text(text):
    words = pos_tag_nltk(text)
    words = \
    [(word_tuple[0], pos_mapping[word_tuple[1]] if \
        word_tuple[1] in pos_mapping.keys() else
        word_tuple[1]) for word_tuple in words]
    words = [(lemmatizer.lemmatize(word_tuple[0]) if \
            word_tuple[1] in accepted_pos else \
            word_tuple[0],
            word_tuple[1]) for word_tuple in words]
    return words
```

4. Read in a text file, in this case, the `sherlock_holmes_1.txt` file, then use the preceding function to lemmatize the words and print them:

```
sherlock_holmes_text = read_text_file("sherlock_holmes_1.
txt")
lem_words = lemmatize_long_text(sherlock_holmes_text)
print(lem_words)
```

The beginning of the result will be as follows:

```
[('To', 'TO'), ('Sherlock', 'NNP'), ('Holmes', 'NNP'),
('she', 'PRP'), ('is', 'v'), ('always', 'RB'), ('_the_',
'a'), ('woman', 'n'), ('.', '.'), ('I', 'PRP'), ('have',
'v'), ('seldom', 'v'), ('heard', 'RB'), ('him', 'PRP'),
('mention', 'VB'), ('her', 'PRP'), ('under', 'IN'),
('any', 'DT'), ('other', 'a'), ('name', 'n'), ('.', '.'),
('In', 'IN'), ('his', 'PRP$'), ('eye', 'n'), ('she',
'PRP'), ('eclipse', 'v'), ('and', 'CC'), ('predominates',
'v'), ('the', 'DT'), ('whole', 'n'), ('of', 'IN'),
('her', 'PRP$'), ('sex', 'n'), ('.', '.'), ...]
```

You will see that, while correctly lemmatizing some words, such as *eyes* and *eclipses*, it leaves others unchanged, for example, *predominates*.

The `lemmatize_long_text` function takes the text and tags it with parts of speech. Then, it replaces the NLTK verb, adjective, and noun tags with the tags that are required for the lemmatizer, and finally lemmatizes words that have those tags.

Removing stopwords

When we work with words, especially if we are considering words' semantics, we sometimes need to exclude some very frequent words that do not bring any substantial meaning to a sentence, words such as *but*, *can*, *we*, and so on. This recipe shows how to do that.

Getting ready...

For this recipe, we will need a list of **stopwords**. We provide a list in the book's GitHub repository. You might find that for your project, you need to customize the list and add or remove words as necessary.

You can also use the `stopwords` list provided with the `nltk` package.

We will be using the Sherlock Holmes text referred to earlier. For this recipe, we will need just the beginning of the book, which can be found in the `sherlock_holmes_1.txt` file.

How to do it...

In the recipe, we will read in the text file, the file with `stopwords`, tokenize the text file, and remove the stopwords from the list:

1. Import the `csv` and `nltk` modules:

    ```
    import csv
    import nltk
    ```

2. Initialize the stopwords list:

    ```
    csv_file="stopwords.csv"
    with open(csv_file, 'r', encoding='utf-8') as fp:
        reader = csv.reader(fp, delimiter=',', quotechar='"')
        stopwords = [row[0] for row in reader]
    ```

3. Alternatively, set the stopwords list to the NLTK list:

```
stopwords = nltk.corpus.stopwords.words('english')
```

> **Information**
>
> Here is a list of languages that NLTK supports for stopwords: Arabic,
> Azerbaijani, Danish, Dutch, English, Finnish, French, German, Greek,
> Hungarian, Italian, Kazakh, Nepali, Norwegian, Portuguese, Romanian,
> Russian, Spanish, Swedish, and Turkish.

4. Read in the text file:

```
file = open(filename, "r", encoding="utf-8")
text = file.read()
```

5. Remove newlines for better readability:

```
text = text.replace("\n", " ")
```

6. Tokenize the text:

```
words = nltk.tokenize.word_tokenize(text)
```

7. Remove the stopwords:

```
words = [word for word in words if word.lower() not in
stopwords]
```

8. The result will be as follows:

```
['Sherlock', 'Holmes', '_the_', 'woman', '.',
'seldom', 'heard', 'mention', '.', 'eyes', 'eclipses',
'predominates', 'sex', '.', 'felt', 'emotion', 'akin',
'Irene', 'Adler', '.', 'emotions', ',', ',', 'abhorrent',
'cold', ',', 'precise', 'admirably', 'balanced', 'mind',
'.', ',', ',', 'reasoning', 'observing', 'machine',
',', 'lover', 'false', 'position', '.', 'spoke',
'softer', 'passions', ',', 'save', 'gibe', 'sneer', '.',
'admirable', 'observer—excellent', 'drawing', 'veil',
'men', ''', 'motives', 'actions', '.', 'trained',
'reasoner', 'admit', 'intrusions', 'delicate', 'finely',
'adjusted', 'temperament', 'introduce', 'distracting',
'factor', 'throw', 'doubt', 'mental', '.', 'Grit',
'sensitive', 'instrument', ',', 'crack', 'high-power',
```

```
'lenses', ',', 'disturbing', 'strong', 'emotion',
'nature', '.', 'woman', ',', 'woman', 'late', 'Irene',
'Adler', ',', 'dubious', 'questionable', 'memory', '.']
```

How it works...

The code filters the stopwords from the text and leaves the words in the text only if they do not appear in the stopwords list.

In *step 1*, we import the csv and NLTK modules. In *step 2*, we read in the stopwords list. We use the csv.reader class to read in the stopwords file, which contains the words, one per line. The csv.reader object returns one list per row, where a row is a line, and we have to take just the first element of the row. Alternatively, in *step 3*, we initialize the stopwords list from the NLTK package.

In *step 4*, we read in the text file. In the optional *step 5*, we remove newlines for better readability. In *step 6*, we tokenize the text and turn it into a list of words. In *step 7*, we create a new list of words that only keeps words that are not in the stopwords list. You will notice that the final line of the code checks whether the *lower-case* version of the word is in the stopwords list, since all the stopwords are lowercase.

> **Important note**
> You might find that some of the words in the stopwords list provided are not necessary or are missing. You will need to modify the list accordingly.

There's more...

We can also compile a stopwords list by using the text we are working with and calculating the frequencies of the words in it. In this section, I will show you two ways of doing so. You will need to use the sherlock_holmes.txt file. The FreqDist object in the NLTK package counts the number of occurrences of each word:

1. Import the nltk module and the FreqDist class:

   ```
   import nltk
   from nltk.probability import FreqDist
   ```

2. Read in the text file:

   ```
   file = open(filename, "r", encoding="utf-8")
   text = file.read()
   ```

3. Remove newlines for better readability:

```
text = text.replace("\n", " ")
```

4. Tokenize the text:

```
words = nltk.tokenize.word_tokenize(text)
```

5. Create the frequency distribution object and use it to create a list of tuples where the first element is the word and the second one is the frequency count:

```
freq_dist = FreqDist(word.lower() for word in words)
words_with_frequencies = \
    [(word, freq_dist[word]) for word in freq_dist.keys()]
```

6. Sort the list of tuples by frequency:

```
sorted_words = sorted(words_with_frequencies,
                    key=lambda tup: tup[1])
```

7. Now we have two options: use a frequency cutoff for the stopwords or take the top n% of words sorted by frequency. Here is the first option. Use 100 as the frequency cutoff:

```
stopwords = [tuple[0] for tuple in sorted_words if
tuple[1] > 100]
```

8. The result is as follows:

```
['away', 'never', 'good', 'nothing', 'case', 'however',
'quite', 'found', 'made', 'house', 'such', 'heard',
'way', 'yes', 'hand', 'much', 'matter', 'where', 'might',
'just', 'room', 'any', 'face', 'here', 'back', 'door',
'how', 'them', 'two', 'other', 'came', 'time', 'did',
'than', 'come', 'before', 'must', 'only', 'know',
'about', 'shall', 'think', 'more', 'over', 'us', 'well',
'am', 'or', 'may', 'they', ';', 'our', 'should', 'now',
'see', 'down', 'can', 'some', 'if', 'will', 'mr.',
'little', 'who', 'into', 'do', 'has', 'could', 'up',
'man', 'out', 'when', 'would', 'an', 'are', 'by', '!',
'were', 's', 'then', 'one', 'all', 'on', 'no', 'what',
'been', 'your', 'very', 'him', 'her', 'she', 'so', '``',
'holmes', 'upon', 'this', 'said', 'from', 'there', 'we',
'me', 'be', 'but', 'not', 'for', '?', 'at', 'which',
'with', 'had', 'as', 'have', 'my', "''", 'is', 'his',
```

```
'was', 'you', 'he', 'it', 'that', 'in', '"', 'a', 'of',
'to', '"', 'and', 'i', '.', 'the', ',']
```

9. The other option is to use the `n%` most frequent words as `stopwords`. Here I use `0.2%` of the most frequent words:

```
length_cutoff = int(0.02*len(sorted_words))
stopwords = [tuple[0] for tuple in sorted_words[-length_
cutoff:]]
```

And the result is as follows:

```
['make', 'myself', 'night', 'until', 'street', 'few',
'why', 'thought', 'take', 'friend', 'lady', 'side',
'small', 'still', 'these', 'find', 'st.', 'every',
'watson', 'too', 'round', 'young', 'father', 'left',
'day', 'yet', 'first', 'once', 'took', 'its', 'eyes',
'long', 'miss', 'through', 'asked', 'most', 'saw',
'oh', 'morning', 'right', 'last', 'like', 'say', 'tell',
't', 'sherlock', 'their', 'go', 'own', 'after', 'away',
'never', 'good', 'nothing', 'case', 'however', 'quite',
'found', 'made', 'house', 'such', 'heard', 'way', 'yes',
'hand', 'much', 'matter', 'where', 'might', 'just',
'room', 'any', 'face', 'here', 'back', 'door', 'how',
'them', 'two', 'other', 'came', 'time', 'did', 'than',
'come', 'before', 'must', 'only', 'know', 'about',
'shall', 'think', 'more', 'over', 'us', 'well', 'am',
'or', 'may', 'they', ';', 'our', 'should', 'now', 'see',
'down', 'can', 'some', 'if', 'will', 'mr.', 'little',
'who', 'into', 'do', 'has', 'could', 'up', 'man', 'out',
'when', 'would', 'an', 'are', 'by', '!', 'were', 's',
'then', 'one', 'all', 'on', 'no', 'what', 'been', 'your',
'very', 'him', 'her', 'she', 'so', "'", 'holmes', 'upon',
'this', 'said', 'from', 'there', 'we', 'me', 'be', 'but',
'not', 'for', '?', 'at', 'which', 'with', 'had', 'as',
'have', 'my', "'", 'is', 'his', 'was', 'you', 'he', 'it',
'that', 'in', '"', 'a', 'of', 'to', '"', 'and', 'i', '.',
'the', ',']
```

You can compare the different stopword lists and pick the one that best suits your needs.

2
Playing with Grammar

Grammar is one of the main building blocks of language. Each human language, and programming language for that matter, has a set of rules that every person speaking it has to follow because otherwise, they risk not being understood. These grammatical rules can be uncovered using NLP and are useful for extracting data from sentences. For example, using information about the grammatical structure of text, we can parse out subjects, objects, and relationships between different entities.

In this chapter, you will learn how to use different packages to reveal the grammatical structure of words and sentences, as well as extract certain parts of sentences. We will cover the following topics:

- Counting nouns – plural and singular nouns
- Getting the dependency parse
- Splitting sentences into clauses
- Extracting noun chunks
- Extracting entities and relations
- Extracting subjects and objects of the sentence
- Finding references – anaphora resolution

Let's get started!

Technical requirements

Follow these steps to install the packages and models required for this chapter:

```
pip install inflect
python -m spacy download en_core_web_md
pip install textacy
```

For the *Finding references: anaphora resolution* recipe, we have to install the `neuralcoref` package. To install this package, use the following command:

```
pip install neuralcoref
```

In case, when running the code, you encounter errors that mention `spacy.strings.StringStore size changed`, you might need to install `neuralcoref` from the source:

```
pip uninstall neuralcoref
git clone https://github.com/huggingface/neuralcoref.git
cd neuralcoref
pip install -r requirements.txt
pip install -e
```

For more information about installation and usage, see `https://github.com/huggingface/neuralcoref`.

Counting nouns – plural and singular nouns

In this recipe, we will do two things:

- Determine whether a noun is plural or singular
- Turn plural nouns into singular nouns and vice versa

You might need these two things in a variety of tasks: in making your chatbot speak in grammatically correct sentences, in coming up with text classification features, and so on.

Getting ready

We will be using `nltk` for this task, as well as the `inflect` module we described in *Technical requirements* section. The code for this chapter is located in the `Chapter02` directory of this book's GitHub repository. We will be working with the first part of the *Adventures of Sherlock Holmes* text, available in the `sherlock_holmes_1.txt` file.

How to do it...

We will be using code from *Chapter 1, Learning NLP Basics*, to tokenize the text into words and tag them with parts of speech. Then, we will use one of two ways to determine if a noun is singular or plural, and then use the `inflect` module to change the number of the noun.

Your steps should be formatted like so:

1. Do the necessary imports:

    ```
    import nltk
    from nltk.stem import WordNetLemmatizer
    import inflect
    from Chapter01.pos_tagging import pos_tag_nltk
    ```

2. Read in the text file:

    ```
    file = open(filename, "r", encoding="utf-8")
    sherlock_holmes_text = file.read()
    ```

3. Remove newlines for better readability:

    ```
    sherlock_holmes_text = sherlock_holmes_text.replace("\n",
    " ")
    ```

4. Do part of speech tagging:

    ```
    words_with_pos = pos_tag_nltk(sherlock_holmes_text)
    ```

5. Define the `get_nouns` function, which will filter out the nouns from all the words:

    ```
    def get_nouns(words_with_pos):
        noun_set = ["NN", "NNS"]
        nouns = [word for word in words_with_pos if
                word[1] in noun_set]
        return nouns
    ```

6. Run the preceding function on the list of POS-tagged words and print it:

```
nouns = get_nouns(words_with_pos)
print(nouns)
```

The resulting list will be as follows:

```
[('woman', 'NN'), ('name', 'NN'), ('eyes', 'NNS'),
('whole', 'NN'), ('sex', 'NN'), ('emotion', 'NN'),
('akin', 'NN'), ('emotions', 'NNS'), ('cold', 'NN'),
('precise', 'NN'), ('mind', 'NN'), ('reasoning',
'NN'), ('machine', 'NN'), ('world', 'NN'), ('lover',
'NN'), ('position', 'NN'), ('passions', 'NNS'),
('gibe', 'NN'), ('sneer', 'NN'), ('things', 'NNS'),
('observer-excellent', 'NN'), ('veil', 'NN'), ('men',
'NNS'), ('motives', 'NNS'), ('actions', 'NNS'),
('reasoner', 'NN'), ('intrusions', 'NNS'), ('delicate',
'NN'), ('temperament', 'NN'), ('distracting', 'NN'),
('factor', 'NN'), ('doubt', 'NN'), ('results', 'NNS'),
('instrument', 'NN'), ('crack', 'NN'), ('high-power',
'NN'), ('lenses', 'NNS'), ('emotion', 'NN'), ('nature',
'NN'), ('woman', 'NN'), ('woman', 'NN'), ('memory',
'NN')]
```

7. To determine whether a noun is singular or plural, we have two options. The first option is to use the NLTK tags, where NN indicates a singular noun and NNS indicates a plural noun. The following function uses the NLTK tags and returns True if the input noun is plural:

```
def is_plural_nltk(noun_info):
    pos = noun_info[1]
    if (pos == "NNS"):
        return True
    else:
        return False
```

8. The other option is to use the WordNetLemmatizer class in the nltk.stem package. The following function returns True if the noun is plural:

```
def is_plural_wn(noun):
    wnl = WordNetLemmatizer()
    lemma = wnl.lemmatize(noun, 'n')
```

```
plural = True if noun is not lemma else False
return plural
```

9. The following function will change a singular noun into plural:

```
def get_plural(singular_noun):
    p = inflect.engine()
    return p.plural(singular_noun)
```

10. The following function will change a plural noun into singular:

```
def get_singular(plural_noun):
    p = inflect.engine()
    plural = p.singular_noun(plural_noun)
    if (plural):
        return plural
    else:
        return plural_noun
```

We can now use the two preceding functions to return a list of nouns changed into plural or singular, depending on the original noun. The following code uses the is_plural_wn function to determine if the noun is plural. You can also use the is_plural_nltk function:

```
def plurals_wn(words_with_pos):
    other_nouns = []
    for noun_info in words_with_pos:
        word = noun_info[0]
        plural = is_plural_wn(word)
        if (plural):
            singular = get_singular(word)
            other_nouns.append(singular)
        else:
            plural = get_plural(word)
            other_nouns.append(plural)
    return other_nouns
```

11. Use the preceding function to return a list of changed nouns:

```
other_nouns_wn = plurals_wn(nouns)
```

The result will be as follows:

```
['women', 'names', 'eye', 'wholes', 'sexes',
 'emotions', 'akins', 'emotion', 'colds', 'precises',
 'minds', 'reasonings', 'machines', 'worlds', 'lovers',
 'positions', 'passion', 'gibes', 'sneers', 'thing',
 'observer-excellents', 'veils', 'mens', 'motive',
 'action', 'reasoners', 'intrusion', 'delicates',
 'temperaments', 'distractings', 'factors', 'doubts',
 'result', 'instruments', 'cracks', 'high-powers', 'lens',
 'emotions', 'natures', 'women', 'women', 'memories']
```

How it works...

Number detection works in one of two ways. One is by reading the part of speech tag assigned by NLTK. If the tag is NN, then the noun is singular, and if it is NNS, then it's plural. The other way is to use the WordNet lemmatizer and to compare the lemma and the original word. The noun is singular if the lemma and the original input noun are the same, and plural otherwise.

To find the singular form of a plural noun and the plural form of a singular noun, we can use the `inflect` package. Its `plural` and `singular_noun` methods return the correct forms.

In *step 1*, we import the necessary modules and functions. You can find the `pos_tag_nltk` function in this book's GitHub repository, in the `Chapter01` module, in the `pos_tagging.py` file It uses the code we wrote for *Chapter 1, Learning NLP Basics*. In *step 2*, we read in the file's contents into a string. In *step 3*, we remove newlines from the text; this is an optional step. In *step 4*, we use the `pos_tag_nltk` function defined in the code from the previous chapter to tag parts of speech for the words.

In *step 5*, we create the `get_nouns` function, which filters out the words that are singular or plural nouns. In this function, we use a list comprehension and keep only words that have the *NN* or *NNS* tags.

In *step 6*, we run the preceding function on the word list and print the result. As you will notice, NLTK tags several words incorrectly as nouns, such as *cold* and *precise*. These errors will propagate into the next steps, and it is something to keep in mind when working with NLP tasks.

In *steps 7* and *8*, we define two functions to determine whether a noun is singular or plural. In *step 7*, we define the `is_plural_nltk` function, which uses NLTK POS tagging information to determine if the noun is plural. In *step 8*, we define the `is_plural_wn` function, which compares the noun with its lemma, as determined by the NLTK lemmatizer. If those two forms are the same, the noun is singular, and if they are different, the noun is plural. Both functions can return incorrect results that will propagate downstream.

In *step 9*, we define the `get_plural` function, which will return the plural form of the noun by using the `inflect` package. In *step 10*, we define the `get_singular` function, which uses the same package to get the singular form of the noun. If there is no output from `inflect`, the function returns the input.

In *step 11*, we define the `plurals_wn` function, which takes in a list of words with the parts of speech that we got in *step 6* and changes plural nouns into singular and singular nouns into plural.

In *step 12*, we run the `plurals_wn` function on the nouns list. Most of the words are changed correctly; for example, *women* and *emotion*. We also see two kinds of error propagation, where either the part of speech or number of the noun were determined incorrectly. For example, the word *akins* appears here because *akin* was incorrectly labeled as a noun. On the other hand, the word *men* was incorrectly determined to be singular and resulted in the wrong output; that is, *mens*.

There's more...

The results will differ, depending on which `is_plural/is_singular` function you use. If you tag the word *men* with its part of speech, you will see that NLTK returns the NNS tag, which means that the word is plural. You can experiment with different inputs and see which function works best for you.

Getting the dependency parse

A dependency parse is a tool that shows dependencies in a sentence. For example, in the sentence *The cat wore a hat*, the root of the sentence in the verb, *wore*, and both the subject, *the cat*, and the object, *a hat*, are dependents. The dependency parse can be very useful in many NLP tasks since it shows the grammatical structure of the sentence, along with the subject, the main verb, the object, and so on. It can be then used in downstream processing.

Getting ready

We will use `spacy` to create the dependency parse. If you already downloaded it while working on the previous chapter, you do not need to do anything more. Otherwise, please follow the instructions at the beginning of *Chapter 1, Learning NLP Basics*, to install the necessary packages.

How to do it...

We will take a few sentences from the `sherlock_holmes1.txt` file to illustrate the dependency parse. The steps are as follows:

1. Import `spacy`:

    ```
    import spacy
    ```

2. Load the sentence to be parsed:

    ```
    sentence = 'I have seldom heard him mention her under any
    other name.'
    ```

3. Load the `spacy` engine:

    ```
    nlp = spacy.load('en_core_web_sm')
    ```

4. Process the sentence using the `spacy` engine:

    ```
    doc = nlp(sentence)
    ```

5. The dependency information will be contained in the `doc` object. We can see the dependency tags by looping through the tokens in `doc`:

    ```
    for token in doc:
        print(token.text, "\t", token.dep_, "\t",
        spacy.explain(token.dep_))
    ```

6. The result will be as follows. To learn what each of the tags means, use spaCy's `explain` function, which shows the meanings of the tags:

I	nsubj	nominal subject	
have	aux	auxiliary	
seldom	advmod		adverbial modifier
heard	ROOT	None	
him	nsubj	nominal subject	

mention		ccomp	clausal complement
her	dobj	direct object	
under	prep	prepositional modifier	
any	det	determiner	
other	amod	adjectival modifier	
name	pobj	object of preposition	
.	punct	punctuation	

7. To explore the dependency parse structure, we can use the attributes of the `Token` class. Using its `ancestors` and `children` attributes, we can get the tokens that this token depends on and the tokens that depend on it, respectively. The code to get these ancestors is as follows:

```
for token in doc:
    print(token.text)
    ancestors = [t.text for t in token.ancestors]
    print(ancestors)
```

The output will be as follows:

```
I
['heard']
have
['heard']
seldom
['heard']
heard
[]
him
['mention', 'heard']
mention
['heard']
her
['mention', 'heard']
under
['mention', 'heard']
any
['name', 'under', 'mention', 'heard']
other
```

```
['name', 'under', 'mention', 'heard']
```
```
name
```
```
['under', 'mention', 'heard']
```
```
.
```
```
['heard']
```

8. To see all the `children token`, use the following code:

```
for token in doc:
    print(token.text)
    children = [t.text for t in token.children]
    print(children)
```

9. The output will be as follows:

```
I
```
```
[]
```
```
have
```
```
[]
```
```
seldom
```
```
[]
```
```
heard
```
```
['I', 'have', 'seldom', 'mention', '.']
```
```
him
```
```
[]
```
```
mention
```
```
['him', 'her', 'under']
```
```
her
```
```
[]
```
```
under
```
```
['name']
```
```
any
```
```
[]
```
```
other
```
```
[]
```

```
name
['any', 'other']
.
[]
```

10. We can also see the subtree that the token is in:

```
for token in doc:
    print(token.text)
    subtree = [t.text for t in token.subtree]
    print(subtree)
```

This will produce the following output:

```
I
['I']
have
['have']
seldom
['seldom']
heard
['I', 'have', 'seldom', 'heard', 'him', 'mention', 'her',
'under', 'any', 'other', 'name', '.']
him
['him']
mention
['him', 'mention', 'her', 'under', 'any', 'other',
'name']
her
['her']
under
['under', 'any', 'other', 'name']
any
['any']
other
['other']
```

```
name
['any', 'other', 'name']
.
['.']
```

How it works...

The spacy NLP engine does the dependency parse as part of its overall analysis. The dependency parse tags explain the role of each word in the sentence. ROOT is the main word that all the other words depend on, usually the verb.

From the subtrees that each word is part of, we can see the grammatical phrases that appear in the sentence, such as the **noun phrase (NP)** *any other name* and **prepositional phrase (PP)** *under any other name*.

The dependency chain can be seen by following the ancestor links for each word. For example, if we look at the word *name*, we will see that its ancestors are *under, mention,* and *heard*. The immediate parent of *name* is *under, under's* parent is *mention,* and *mention's* parent is *heard*. A dependency chain will always lead to the root, or the main word, of the sentence.

In *step 1*, we import the spacy package. In *step 2*, we initialize the variable sentence that contains the sentence to be parsed. In *step 3*, we load the spacy engine and in *step 4*, we use the engine to process the sentence.

In *step 5*, we print out each token's dependency tag and use the spacy.explain function to see what those tags mean.

In *step 6*, we print out the ancestors of each token. The ancestors will start at the parent and go up until they reach the root. For example, the parent of *him* is *mention,* and the parent of *mention* is *heard,* so both *mention* and *heard* are listed as ancestors of *him*.

In *step 7*, we print children of each token. Some tokens, such as *have,* do not have any children, while others have several. The token that will always have children, unless the sentence consists of one word, is the root of the sentence; in this case, *heard*.

In *step 8*, we print the subtree for each token. For example, the word *under* is in the subtree *under any other name*.

See also

The dependency parse can be visualized graphically using the `displacy` package, which is part of `spacy`. Please see *Chapter 8, Visualizing Text Data*, for a detailed recipe on how to perform visualization.

Splitting sentences into clauses

When we work with text, we frequently deal with compound (sentences with two parts that are equally important) and complex sentences (sentences with one part depending on another). It is sometimes useful to split these composite sentences into its component clauses for easier processing down the line. This recipe uses the dependency parse from the previous recipe.

Getting ready

You will only need the `spacy` package in this recipe.

How to do it...

We will work with two sentences, *He eats cheese, but he won't eat ice cream* and *If it rains later, we won't be able to go to the park*. Other sentences may turn out to be more complicated to deal with, and I leave it as an exercise for you to split such sentences. Follow these steps:

1. Import the `spacy` package:

    ```
    import spacy
    ```

2. Load the `spacy` engine:

    ```
    nlp = spacy.load('en_core_web_sm')
    ```

3. Set the sentence to `He eats cheese, but he won't eat ice cream`:

    ```
    sentence = "He eats cheese, but he won't eat ice cream."
    ```

4. Process the sentence with the `spacy` engine:

    ```
    doc = nlp(sentence)
    ```

5. It is instructive to look at the structure of the input sentence by printing out the part of speech, dependency tag, ancestors, and children of each token. This can be accomplished using the following code:

```
for token in doc:
    ancestors = [t.text for t in token.ancestors]
    children = [t.text for t in token.children]
    print(token.text, "\t", token.i, "\t",
        token.pos_, "\t", token.dep_, "\t",
        ancestors, "\t", children)
```

6. We will use the following function to find the root token of the sentence, which is usually the main verb. In instances where there is a dependent clause, it is the verb of the independent clause:

```
def find_root_of_sentence(doc):
    root_token = None
    for token in doc:
        if (token.dep_ == "ROOT"):
            root_token = token
    return root_token
```

7. We will now find the root token of the sentence:

```
root_token = find_root_of_sentence(doc)
```

8. We can now use the following function to find the other verbs in the sentence:

```
def find_other_verbs(doc, root_token):
    other_verbs = []
    for token in doc:
        ancestors = list(token.ancestors)
        if (token.pos_ == "VERB" and len(ancestors) == 1\
            and ancestors[0] == root_token):
            other_verbs.append(token)
    return other_verbs
```

9. Use the preceding function to find the remaining verbs in the sentence:

```
other_verbs = find_other_verbs(doc, root_token)
```

We will use the following function to find the token spans for each verb:

```
def get_clause_token_span_for_verb(verb, doc, all_verbs):
    first_token_index = len(doc)
    last_token_index = 0
    this_verb_children = list(verb.children)
    for child in this_verb_children:
        if (child not in all_verbs):
            if (child.i < first_token_index):
                first_token_index = child.i
            if (child.i > last_token_index):
                last_token_index = child.i
    return(first_token_index, last_token_index)
```

10. We will put together all the verbs in one array and process each using the preceding function. This will return a tuple of start and end indices for each verb's clause:

```
token_spans = []
all_verbs = [root_token] + other_verbs
for other_verb in all_verbs:
    (first_token_index, last_token_index) = \
     get_clause_token_span_for_verb(other_verb,
                                    doc, all_verbs)
    token_spans.append((first_token_index,
                        last_token_index))
```

11. Using the start and end indices, we can now put together token spans for each clause. We sort the sentence_clauses list at the end so that the clauses are in the order they appear in the sentence:

```
sentence_clauses = []
for token_span in token_spans:
    start = token_span[0]
    end = token_span[1]
    if (start < end):
        clause = doc[start:end]
        sentence_clauses.append(clause)
sentence_clauses = sorted(sentence_clauses,
                          key=lambda tup: tup[0])
```

12. Now, we can print the final result of the processing for our initial sentence; that is,
    `He eats cheese, but he won't eat ice cream`:

```
clauses_text = [clause.text for clause in sentence_
clauses]
print(clauses_text)
```

The result is as follows:

```
['He eats cheese,', 'he won't eat ice cream']
```

> **Important note**
> The code in this section will work for some cases, but not others; I encourage
> you to test it out on different cases and amend the code.

How it works...

The way the code works is based on the way complex and compound sentences are
structured. Each clause contains a verb, and one of the verbs is the main verb of the
sentence (root). The code looks for the root verb, always marked with the ROOT
dependency tag in spaCy processing, and then looks for the other verbs in the sentence.

The code then uses the information about each verb's children to find the left and right
boundaries of the clause. Using this information, the code then constructs the text of the
clauses. A step-by-step explanation follows.

In *step 1*, we import the spaCy package and in *step 2*, we load the spacy engine. In *step
3*, we set the sentence variable and in *step 4*, we process it using the spacy engine. In *step
5*, we print out the dependency parse information. It will help us determine how to split
the sentence into clauses.

In *step 6*, we define the `find_root_of_sentence` function, which returns the token
that has a dependency tag of ROOT. In *step 7*, we find the root of the sentence we are using
as an example.

In *step 8*, we define the `find_other_verbs` function, which will find other verbs in the
sentence. In this function, we look for tokens that have the VERB part of speech tag and
has the root token as its only ancestor. In *step 9*, we apply this function.

In *step 10*, we define the `get_clause_token_span_for_verb` function, which will
find the beginning and ending index for the verb. The function goes through all the verb's
children; the leftmost child's index is the beginning index, while the rightmost child's
index is the ending index for this verb's clause.

In *step 11*, we use the preceding function to find the clause indices for each verb. The `token_spans` variable contains the list of tuples, where the first tuple element is the beginning clause index and the second tuple element is the ending clause index.

In *step 12*, we create token `Span` objects for each clause in the sentence using the list of beginning and ending index pairs we created in *step 11*. We get the `Span` object by slicing the `Doc` object and then appending the resulting `Span` objects to a list. As a final step, we sort the list to make sure that the clauses in the list are in the same order as in the sentence.

In *step 13*, we print the clauses in our sentence. You will notice that the word *but* is missing, since its parent is the root verb *eats*, although it appears in the other clause. The exercise of including *but* is left to you.

Extracting noun chunks

Noun chunks are known in linguistics as **noun phrases**. They represent nouns and any words that depend on and accompany nouns. For example, in the sentence *The big red apple fell on the scared cat*, the noun chunks are *the big red apple* and *the scared cat*. Extracting these noun chunks is instrumental to many other downstream NLP tasks, such as named entity recognition and processing entities and relationships between them. In this recipe, we will explore how to extract named entities from a piece of text.

Getting ready

We will be using the `spacy` package, which has a function for extracting noun chunks and the text from the `sherlock_holmes_1.txt` file as an example.

In this section, we will use another spaCy language model, `en_core_web_md`. Follow the instructions in the *Technical requirements* section to learn how to download it.

How to do it...

Use the following steps to get the noun chunks from a piece of text:

1. Import the `spacy` package and the `read_text_file` from the code files of chapter 1:

```
import spacy
from Chapter01.dividing_into_sentences import read_text_
file
```

> **Important note**
> If you are importing functions from other chapters, run it from the directory
> that precedes Chapter02 and use the `python -m Chapter02.`
> `extract_noun_chunks` command.

2. Read in the `sherlock_holmes_1.txt` file:

```
text = read_text_file("sherlock_holmes_1.txt")
```

3. Initialize the `spacy` engine and then use it to process the text:

```
nlp = spacy.load('en_core_web_md')
doc = nlp(text)
```

4. The noun chunks are contained in the `doc.noun_chunks` class variable. We can
    print out the chunks:

```
for noun_chunk in doc.noun_chunks:
    print(noun_chunk.text)
```

This is the partial result. See this book's GitHub repository for the full printout,
which can be found in the `Chapter02/all_text_noun_chunks.txt` file:

```
Sherlock Holmes
she
the_ woman
I
him
her
any other name
his eyes
she
the whole
...
```

How it works...

The spaCy Doc object, as we saw in the previous recipe, contains information about
grammatical relationships between words in a sentence. Using this information, spaCy
determines noun phrases or chunks contained in the text.

In *step 1*, we import spacy and the `read_text_file` function from the `Chapter01` module. In *step 2*, we read in the text from the `sherlock_holmes_1.txt` file.

In *step 3*, we initialize the `spacy` engine with a different model, en_core_web_md, which is larger and will most likely give better results. There is also the large model, en_core_web_lg, which is even larger. It will give better results, but the processing will be slower. After loading the engine, we run it on the text we loaded in *step 2*.

In *step 4*, we print out the noun chunks that appear in the text. As you can see, it gets the pronouns, nouns, and noun phrases that are in the text correctly.

There's more...

Noun chunks are spaCy `Span` objects and have all their properties. See the official documentation at `https://spacy.io/api/token`.

Let's explore some properties of noun chunks:

1. Import the `spacy` package:

    ```
    import spacy
    ```

2. Load the `spacy` engine:

    ```
    nlp = spacy.load('en_core_web_sm')
    ```

3. Set the sentence to *All emotions, and that one particularly, were abhorrent to his cold, precise but admirably balanced mind*:

    ```
    sentence = "All emotions, and that one particularly, were
    abhorrent to his cold, precise but admirably balanced
    mind."
    ```

4. Process the sentence with the `spacy` engine:

    ```
    doc = nlp(sentence)
    ```

5. Let's look at the noun chunks in this sentence:

    ```
    for noun_chunk in doc.noun_chunks:
        print(noun_chunk.text)
    ```

6. This is the result:

    ```
    All emotions
    his cold, precise but admirably balanced mind
    ```

7. Some of the basic properties of noun chunks are its start and end offsets; we can print them out together with the noun chunks:

```
for noun_chunk in doc.noun_chunks:
    print(noun_chunk.text, "\t", noun_chunk.start, "\t",
        noun_chunk.end)
```

The result will be as follows:

```
All emotions      0        2
his cold, precise but admirably balanced mind      11
19
```

8. We can also print out the sentence where the noun chunk belongs:

```
for noun_chunk in doc.noun_chunks:
    print(noun_chunk.text, "\t", noun_chunk.sent)
```

Predictably, this results in the following:

```
All emotions      All emotions, and that one particularly,
were abhorrent to his cold, precise but admirably
balanced mind.
his cold, precise but admirably balanced mind      All
emotions, and that one particularly, were abhorrent to
his cold, precise but admirably balanced mind.
```

9. Just like a sentence, any noun chunk includes a root, which is the token that all other tokens depend on. In a noun phrase, that is the noun:

```
for noun_chunk in doc.noun_chunks:
    print(noun_chunk.text, "\t", noun_chunk.root.text)
```

10. The result will be as follows:

```
All emotions      emotions
his cold, precise but admirably balanced mind      mind
```

11. Another very useful property of Span is similarity, which is the semantic similarity of different texts. Let's try it out. We will load another noun chunk, emotions, and process it using spacy:

```
other_span = "emotions"
other_doc = nlp(other_span)
```

12. We can now compare it to the noun chunks in the sentence by using this code:

```
for noun_chunk in doc.noun_chunks:
    print(noun_chunk.similarity(other_doc))
```

This is the result:

```
UserWarning: [W007] The model you're using has no word
vectors loaded, so the result of the Span.similarity
method will be based on the tagger, parser and NER, which
may not give useful similarity judgements. This may
happen if you're using one of the small models, e.g. `en_
core_web_sm`, which don't ship with word vectors and only
use context-sensitive tensors. You can always add your
own word vectors, or use one of the larger models instead
if available.
    print(noun_chunk.similarity(other_doc))
All emotions
0.373233604751925
his cold, precise but admirably balanced mind
0.030945358271699138
```

13. Although the result makes sense, with *all emotions* being more similar to *emotions* than to *his cold, precise but admirably balanced mind*, we get a warning. In order to fix this, we will use the medium `spacy` model, which contains vector representations for words. Substitute this line for the line in *step 2*; the rest of the code will remain the same:

```
nlp = spacy.load('en_core_web_md')
```

14. Now, when we run this code with the new model, we get this result:

```
All emotions
0.8876554549427152
that one
0.37378867755652434
his cold, precise but admirably balanced mind
0.5102475977383759
```

The result shows the similarity of `all emotions` to `emotions` being very high, 0.89, and to `his cold, precise but admirably balanced mind`, 0.51. We can also see that the larger model detects another noun chunk, *that one*.

> **Important note**
> A larger `spaCy` model, such as `en_core_web_md`, takes up more space, but is more precise.

See also

The topic of semantic similarity will be explored in more detail in *Chapter 3, Representing Text: Capturing Semantics*.

Extracting entities and relations

It is possible to extract triplets of the subject entity-relation-object entity from documents, which are frequently used in knowledge graphs. These triplets can then be analyzed for further relations and inform other NLP tasks, such as searches.

Getting ready

For this recipe, we will need another Python package based on `spacy`, called `textacy`. The main advantage of this package is that it allows regular expression-like searching for tokens based on their part of speech tags. See the installation instructions in the *Technical requirements* section at the beginning of this chapter for more information.

How to do it...

We will find all verb phrases in the text, as well as all the noun phrases (see the previous section). Then, we will find the left noun phrase (subject) and the right noun phrase (object) that relate to a particular verb phrase. We will use two simple sentences, *All living things are made of cells* and *Cells have organelles*. Follow these steps:

1. Import `spaCy` and `textacy`:

```
import spacy
import textacy
from Chapter02.split_into_clauses import find_root_of_
sentence
```

2. Load the `spacy` engine:

```
nlp = spacy.load('en_core_web_sm')
```

3. We will get a list of sentences that we will be processing:

```
sentences = ["All living things are made of cells.",
             "Cells have organelles."]
```

4. In order to find verb phrases, we will need to compile regular expression-like patterns for the part of speech combinations of the words that make up the verb phrase. If we print out parts of speech of verb phrases of the two preceding sentences, *are made of and have*, we will see that the part of speech sequences are AUX, VERB, ADP, and AUX.

```
verb_patterns = [[{"POS":"AUX"}, {"POS":"VERB"},
                  {"POS":"ADP"}],
                 [{"POS":"AUX"}]]
```

5. The `contains_root` function checks if a verb phrase contains the root of the sentence:

```
def contains_root(verb_phrase, root):
    vp_start = verb_phrase.start
    vp_end = verb_phrase.end
    if (root.i >= vp_start and root.i <= vp_end):
        return True
    else:
        return False
```

6. The `get_verb_phrases` function gets the verb phrases from a spaCy `Doc` object:

```
def get_verb_phrases(doc):
    root = find_root_of_sentence(doc)
    verb_phrases = textacy.extract.matches(doc,
                                           verb_patterns)
    new_vps = []
    for verb_phrase in verb_phrases:
        if (contains_root(verb_phrase, root)):
            new_vps.append(verb_phrase)
    return new_vps
```

7. The `longer_verb_phrase` function finds the longest verb phrase:

```
def longer_verb_phrase(verb_phrases):
    longest_length = 0
    longest_verb_phrase = None
    for verb_phrase in verb_phrases:
        if len(verb_phrase) > longest_length:
            longest_verb_phrase = verb_phrase
    return longest_verb_phrase
```

8. The `find_noun_phrase` function will look for noun phrases either on the left- or right-hand side of the main verb phrase:

```
def find_noun_phrase(verb_phrase, noun_phrases, side):
    for noun_phrase in noun_phrases:
        if (side == "left" and \
            noun_phrase.start < verb_phrase.start):
            return noun_phrase
        elif (side == "right" and \
              noun_phrase.start > verb_phrase.start):
            return noun_phrase
```

9. In this function, we will use the preceding functions to find triplets of subject-relation-object in the sentences:

```
def find_triplet(sentence):
    doc = nlp(sentence)
    verb_phrases = get_verb_phrases(doc)
    noun_phrases = doc.noun_chunks
    verb_phrase = None
    if (len(verb_phrases) > 1):
        verb_phrase = \
        longer_verb_phrase(list(verb_phrases))
    else:
        verb_phrase = verb_phrases[0]
    left_noun_phrase = find_noun_phrase(verb_phrase,
                                        noun_phrases,
                                        "left")
    right_noun_phrase = find_noun_phrase(verb_phrase,
```

```
                                        noun_phrases,
                                            "right")
        return (left_noun_phrase, verb_phrase,
                right_noun_phrase)
```

10. We can now loop through our sentence list to find its relation triplets:

```
for sentence in sentences:
    (left_np, vp, right_np) = find_triplet(sentence)
    print(left_np, "\t", vp, "\t", right_np)
```

11. The result will be as follows:

```
All living things      are made of      cells
Cells    have    organelles
```

How it works...

The code finds triplets of subject-relation-object by looking for the root verb phrase and finding its surrounding nouns. The verb phrases are found using the `textacy` package, which provides a very useful tool for finding patterns of words of certain parts of speech. In effect, we can use it to write small grammars describing the necessary phrases.

> **Important note**
> The `textacy` package, while very useful, is not bug-free, so use it with caution.

Once the verb phrases have been found, we can prune through the sentence noun chunks to find those that are around the verb phrase containing the root.

A step-by-step explanation follows.

In *step 1*, we import the necessary packages and the `find_root_of_sentence` function from the previous recipe. In *step 2*, we initialize the `spacy` engine, and in *step 3*, we initialize a list with the sentences we will be using.

In *step 4*, we compile part of speech patterns that we will use for finding relations. For these two sentences, the patterns are AUX, VERB, ADP, and AUX.

In *step 5*, we create the `contains_root` function, which will make sure that a verb phrase contains the root of the sentence. It does that by checking the index of the root and making sure that it falls within the verb phrase span boundaries.

In *step 6*, we create the `get_verb_phrases` function, which extracts all the verb phrases from the `Doc` object that is passed in. It uses the part of speech patterns we created in *step 4*.

In *step 7*, we create the `longer_verb_phrase` function, which will find the longest verb phrase from a list. We do this because some verb phrases might be shorter than necessary. For example, in the sentence *All living things are made of cells*, both *are* and *are made of* will be found.

In *step 8*, we create the `find_noun_phrase` function, which finds noun phrases on either side of the verb. We specify the side as a parameter.

In *step 9*, we create the `find_triplet` function, which will find triplets of subject-relation-object in a sentence. In this function, first, we process the sentence with spaCy. Then, we use the functions defined in the previous steps to find the longest verb phrase and the nouns to the left- and right-hand sides of it.

In *step 10*, we apply the `find_triplet` function to the two sentences we defined at the beginning. The resulting triplets are correct.

In this recipe, we made a few assumptions that will not always be correct. The first assumption is that there will only be one main verb phrase. The second assumption is that there will be a noun chunk on either side of the verb phrase. Once we start working with sentences that are complex or compound, or contain relative clauses, these assumptions no longer hold. I leave it as an exercise for you to work with more complex cases.

There's more...

Once you've parsed out the entities and relations, you might want to input them into a knowledge graph for further use. There are a variety of tools you can use to work with knowledge graphs, such as *neo4j*.

Extracting subjects and objects of the sentence

Sometimes, we might need to find the subject and direct objects of the sentence, and that can easily be accomplished with the `spacy` package.

Getting ready

We will be using the dependency tags from `spacy` to find subjects and objects.

How to do it...

We will use the subtree attribute of tokens to find the complete noun chunk that is the subject or direct object of the verb (see the *Getting the dependency parse* recipe for more information). Let's get started:

1. Import spacy:

    ```
    import spacy
    ```

2. Load the spacy engine:

    ```
    nlp = spacy.load('en_core_web_sm')
    ```

3. We will get the list of sentences we will be processing:

    ```
    sentences=["The big black cat stared at the small dog.",
               "Jane watched her brother in the evenings."]
    ```

4. We will use two functions to find the subject and the direct object of the sentence. These functions will loop through the tokens and return the subtree that contains the token with subj or dobj in the dependency tag, respectively. Here is the subject function:

    ```
    def get_subject_phrase(doc):
        for token in doc:
            if ("subj" in token.dep_):
                subtree = list(token.subtree)
                start = subtree[0].i
                end = subtree[-1].i + 1
                return doc[start:end]
    ```

5. Here is the direct object function. If the sentence does not have a direct object, it will return None:

    ```
    def get_object_phrase(doc):
        for token in doc:
            if ("dobj" in token.dep_):
                subtree = list(token.subtree)
                start = subtree[0].i
    ```

```
            end = subtree[-1].i + 1
            return doc[start:end]
```

6. We can now loop through the sentences and print out their subjects and objects:

```
for sentence in sentences:
    doc = nlp(sentence)
    subject_phrase = get_subject_phrase(doc)
    object_phrase = get_object_phrase(doc)
    print(subject_phrase)
    print(object_phrase)
```

The result will be as follows. Since the first sentence does not have a direct object, None is printed out:

```
The big black cat
None
Jane
her brother
```

How it works...

The code uses the spacy engine to parse the sentence. Then, the subject function loops through the tokens, and if the dependency tag contains subj, it returns that token's subtree, which is a Span object. There are different subject tags, including nsubj for regular subjects and nsubjpass for subjects of passive sentences, so we want to look for both.

The object function works exactly the same as the subject function, except it looks for the token that has dobj (direct object) in its dependency tag. Since not all sentences have direct objects, it returns None in those cases.

In *step 1*, we import spaCy, and in *step 2*, we load the spacy engine. In *step 3*, we initialize a list with the sentences we will be processing.

In *step 4*, we create the get_subject_phrase function, which gets the subject of the sentence. It looks for the token that has a dependency tag that contains subj and then returns the subtree that contains that token. There are several subject dependency tags, including nsubj and nsubjpass (for a subject of a passive sentence), so we look for the most general pattern.

In *step 5*, we create the `get_object_phrase` function, which gets the direct object of the sentence. It works similarly to the `get_subject_phrase`, but looks for the *dobj* dependency tag instead of a tag that contains *"subj"*.

In *step 6*, we loop through the list of sentences we created in *step 3*, and use the preceding functions to find the subjects and direct objects in the sentences. For the sentence *The big black cat stared at the small dog*, the subject is *the big black cat*, and there is no direct object (*the small dog* is the object of the preposition *at*). For the sentence *Jane watched her brother in the evenings*, the subject is *Jane* and the direct object is *her brother*.

There's more...

We can look for other objects; for example, the dative objects of verbs such as *give* and objects of prepositional phrases. The functions will look very similar, with the main difference being the dependency tags; that is, `dative` for the dative object function and `pobj` for the prepositional object function. The prepositional object function will return a list since there can be more than one prepositional phrase in a sentence. Let's take a look:

1. The dative object function checks the tokens for the `dative` tag. It returns `None` if there are no dative objects:

```
def get_dative_phrase(doc):
    for token in doc:
        if ("dative" in token.dep_):
            subtree = list(token.subtree)
            start = subtree[0].i
            end = subtree[-1].i + 1
            return doc[start:end]
```

2. Here is the prepositional object function. It returns a list of objects of prepositions, but will be empty if there are none:

```
def get_prepositional_phrase_objs(doc):
    prep_spans = []
    for token in doc:
        if ("pobj" in token.dep_):
            subtree = list(token.subtree)
            start = subtree[0].i
            end = subtree[-1].i + 1
            prep_spans.append(doc[start:end])
    return prep_spans
```

3. The prepositional phrase objects in the sentence *Jane watched her brother in the evenings* are as follows:

```
[the evenings]
```

4. And here is the dative object in the sentence *Laura gave Sam a very interesting book*:

```
Sam
```

It is left as an exercise for you to find the actual prepositional phrases with prepositions intact instead of just the noun phrases that are dependent on these prepositions.

Finding references – anaphora resolution

When we work on problems of extracting entities and relations from text (see the *Extracting entities and relations* recipe), we are faced with real text, and many of our entities might end up being extracted as pronouns, such as *she* or *him*. In order to tackle this issue, we need to perform **anaphora resolution**, or the process of substituting the pronouns with their referents.

Getting ready

For this task, we will be using a spaCy extension written by *Hugging Face* called neuralcoref (see https://github.com/huggingface/neuralcoref). As the name suggests, it uses neural networks to resolve pronouns. To install the package, use the following command:

```
pip install neuralcoref
```

How to do it...

Your steps should be formatted like so:

1. Import spacy and neuralcoref:

```
import spacy
import neuralcoref
```

2. Load the spaCy engine and add neuralcoref to its pipeline:

```
nlp = spacy.load('en_core_web_sm')
neuralcoref.add_to_pipe(nlp)
```

3. We will process the following short text:

```
text = "Earlier this year, Olga appeared on a new song.
She was featured on one of the tracks. The singer is
assuring that her next album will be worth the wait."
```

4. Now that `neuralcoref` is part of the pipeline, we just process the text using spaCy and then output the result:

```
doc = nlp(text)
print(doc._.coref_resolved)
```

The output will be as follows:

```
Earlier this year, Olga appeared on a new song. Olga was
featured on one of the tracks. Olga is assuring that Olga
next album will be worth the wait.
```

How it works...

In *step 1*, we import the necessary packages. In *step 2*, we load the spacy engine and then add `neuralcoref` to its pipeline. In *step 3*, we initialize the `text` variable with the short text we will be using.

In *step 4*, we use the spacy engine to process the text and then print out the text with the pronouns resolved. You can see that the pronouns *she* and *her*, and even the phrase The singer, were all correctly substituted with the name Olga.

The `neuralcoref` package uses custom spacy attributes that are set by using an underscore and the attribute name. The `coref_resolved` variable is a custom attribute that is set on a Doc object. To learn more about spaCy custom attributes, see https://spacy.io/usage/processing-pipelines#custom-components-attributes.

There's more...

The `neuralcoref` package did a good job of recognizing different references to Olga in the previous section. However, if we use an unusual name, it might not work correctly. Here, we are using an example from the Hugging Face GitHub:

1. Let's use the following short text:

```
text = "Deepika has a dog. She loves him. The movie star
has always been fond of animals."
```

2. Upon processing this text using the preceding code, we get the following output:

```
Deepika has a dog. Deepika loves Deepika. Deepika has
always been fond of animals.
```

3. Because the name *Deepika* is an unusual name, the model has trouble figuring out whether this person is a man or a woman and resolves the pronoun *him* to *Deepika*, although it is incorrect. In order to solve this problem, we can help it by characterizing who *Deepika* actually is. We will add `neuralcoref` to the `spacy` pipe, as follows:

```
neuralcoref.add_to_pipe(nlp, conv_dict={'Deepika':
['woman']})
```

4. Now, let's process the result, as we did previously:

```
doc = nlp(text)
```
```
print(doc._.coref_resolved)
```

The output will be as follows:

```
Deepika has a dog. Deepika loves a dog. Deepika has
always been fond of animals.
```

Once we give the coreference resolution module more information, it gives the correct output.

3
Representing Text – Capturing Semantics

Representing the meaning of words, phrases, and sentences in a form that's understandable to computers is one of the pillars of NLP processing. Machine learning, for example, represents each data point as a fixed-size vector, and we are faced with the question of how to turn words and sentences into vectors. Almost any NLP task starts with representing the text in some numeric form, and this chapter will show several ways of doing that. Once you've learned how to represent text as vectors, you will be able to perform tasks such as classification, which will be described in later chapters.

We will also learn how to turn phrases such as **fried chicken** into vectors, how to train a `word2vec` model, and how to create a small search engine with semantic search.

The following recipes will be covered in this chapter:

- Putting documents into a bag of words
- Constructing the N-gram model
- Representing texts with TF-IDF
- Using word embeddings
- Training your own embeddings model

- Representing phrases – phrase2vec
- Using BERT instead of word embeddings
- Getting started with semantic search

Let's get started!

Technical requirements

The code for this chapter is located at `https://github.com/PacktPublishing/Python-Natural-Language-Processing-Cookbook/tree/master/Chapter03`. In this chapter, we will need additional packages. The installation instructions for Anaconda are as follows:

```
pip install sklearn
pip install gensim
pip install pickle
pip install langdetect
conda install pytorch torchvision cudatoolkit=10.2 -c pytorch
pip install transformers
pip install -U sentence-transformers
pip install whoosh
```

In addition, we will use the models and datasets located at the following URLs:

- `http://vectors.nlpl.eu/repository/20/40.zip`
- `https://www.kaggle.com/currie32/project-gutenbergs-top-20-books`
- `https://www.yelp.com/dataset`
- `https://www.kaggle.com/PromptCloudHQ/imdb-data`

Putting documents into a bag of words

A bag of words is the simplest way of representing text. We treat our text as a collection of documents, where documents are anything from sentences to book chapters to whole books. Since we usually compare different documents to each other or use them in a larger context of other documents, typically, we work with a collection of documents, not just a single document.

The bag of words method uses a training text that provides it with a list of words that it should consider. When encoding new sentences, it counts the number of occurrences each word makes in the document, and the final vector includes those counts for each word in the vocabulary. This representation can then be fed into a machine learning algorithm.

The decision of what represents a document lies with the engineer, and in many cases will be obvious. For example, if you are working on classifying tweets as belonging to a particular topic, a single tweet will be your document. If, on the other hand, you would like to find out which of the chapters of a book are most similar to a book you already have, then chapters are documents.

In this recipe, we will create a bag of words for the beginning of the Sherlock Holmes text. Our documents will be the sentences in the text.

Getting ready

For this recipe, we will be using the CountVectorizer class from the sklearn package. To install the package, use the following command:

```
pip install sklearn
```

Let's begin.

How to do it...

Our code will take a set of documents – sentences, in this case – and represent them as a matrix of vectors. We will use the file sherlock_holmes_1.txt for this task:

1. Import the CountVectorizer class and helper functions from *Chapter 1, Learning NLP Basics*:

```
from sklearn.feature_extraction.text import
CountVectorizer
from Chapter01.dividing_into_sentences import read_text_
file,\
preprocess_text, divide_into_sentences_nltk
```

2. Define the get_sentences function, which will read in the text file, preprocess the text, and divide it into sentences:

```
def get_sentences(filename):
    sherlock_holmes_text = read_text_file(filename)
    sherlock_holmes_text = \
```

```
    preprocess_text(sherlock_holmes_text)
    sentences = \
        divide_into_sentences_nltk(sherlock_holmes_text)
    return sentences
```

3. Create a function that will return the vectorizer and the final matrix:

```
def create_vectorizer(sentences):
    vectorizer = CountVectorizer()
    X = vectorizer.fit_transform(sentences)
    return (vectorizer, X)
```

4. Now, use the aforementioned functions on the sherlock_holmes_1.txt file:

```
sentences = get_sentences("sherlock_holmes_1.txt")
(vectorizer, X) = create_vectorizer(sentences)
```

5. We will now print the matrix representation of the text:

```
print(X)
```

6. The resulting matrix is a scipy.sparse.csr.csr_matrix object, and the beginning of its printout looks like this:

```
    (0, 114)        1
    (0, 99)         1
    (0, 47)         1
    (0, 98)         1
    (0, 54)         1
    (0, 10)         1
    (0, 0)          1
    (0, 124)        1
    ...
```

7. It can also be turned into a numpy.matrixlib.defmatrix.matrix object, where each sentence is a vector. These sentence vectors can be used our machine learning algorithms later:

```
denseX = X.todense()
```

8. Let's print the resulting matrix:

```
print(denseX)
```

9. Its printout looks like this:

```
[[1 0 0 ... 0 0 0]
 [0 0 0 ... 0 0 0]
 [0 0 0 ... 0 0 0]
 ...
 [0 0 0 ... 0 0 0]
 [0 0 0 ... 0 1 0]
 [0 0 0 ... 0 0 1]]
```

10. We can see all the words that were used in the document set:

```
print(vectorizer.get_feature_names())
```

11. The result will be as follows:

```
['_the_', 'abhorrent', 'actions', 'adjusted', 'adler',
'admirable', 'admirably', 'admit', 'akin', 'all',
'always', 'and', 'any', 'as', 'balanced', 'be',
'but', 'cold', 'crack', 'delicate', 'distracting',
'disturbing', 'doubt', 'drawing', 'dubious', 'eclipses',
'emotion', 'emotions', 'excellent', 'eyes', 'factor',
'false', 'felt', 'finely', 'for', 'from', 'gibe',
'grit', 'has', 'have', 'he', 'heard', 'her', 'high',
'him', 'himself', 'his', 'holmes', 'in', 'instrument',
'into', 'introduce', 'intrusions', 'irene', 'is',
'it', 'late', 'lenses', 'love', 'lover', 'machine',
'memory', 'men', 'mental', 'mention', 'might', 'mind',
'more', 'most', 'motives', 'name', 'nature', 'never',
'not', 'observer', 'observing', 'of', 'one', 'or',
'other', 'own', 'particularly', 'passions', 'perfect',
'placed', 'position', 'power', 'precise', 'predominates',
'questionable', 'reasoner', 'reasoning', 'results',
'save', 'seen', 'seldom', 'sensitive', 'sex', 'she',
'sherlock', 'sneer', 'softer', 'spoke', 'strong', 'such',
'take', 'temperament', 'than', 'that', 'the', 'there',
'they', 'things', 'throw', 'to', 'trained', 'under',
'upon', 'veil', 'was', 'were', 'which', 'whole', 'with',
'woman', 'world', 'would', 'yet']
```

12. We can now also use the `CountVectorizer` object to represent new sentences that were not in the original document set. We will use the sentence *I had seen little of Holmes lately*, which is the next sentence after the excerpt in `sherlock_holmes_1.txt`. The `transform` function expects a list of documents, so we will create a new list with the sentence as the only element:

```
new_sentence = "I had seen little of Holmes lately."
new_sentence_vector = vectorizer.transform([new_
sentence])
```

13. We can now print the sparse and dense matrices of this new sentence:

```
print(new_sentence_vector)
print(new_sentence_vector.todense())
```

14. The result will be as follows:

```
  (0, 47)        1
  (0, 76)        1
  (0, 94)        1
[[0 0 0 0 0 0 0 0 0 0 0 0 0 0 0 0 0 0 0 0 0 0 0 0 0 0 0 0 0 0
  0 0 0 0 0 0 0 0
   0 0 0 0 0 0 0 0 0 0 0 1 0 0 0 0 0 0 0 0 0 0 0 0 0 0 0 0 0 0
  0 0 0 0 0 0 0 0
   0 0 0 0 1 0 0 0 0 0 0 0 0 0 0 0 0 0 0 0 0 0 0 1 0 0 0 0 0
  0 0 0 0 0 0 0 0
   0 0 0 0 0 0 0 0 0 0 0 0 0 0 0 0 0 0 0 0]]
```

> **Important Note**
>
> When running the code from this book's GitHub repository, run it like `python -m Chapter03.bag_of_words`. This will ensure the code you've imported from previous chapters works properly.

How it works...

In *step 1*, we import the CountVectorizer class and helper functions. In *step 2*, we define the get_sentences function, which reads the text of a file into a string, preprocesses it, and divides into sentences. In *step 3*, we define the create_vectorizer function, which takes in a list of sentences and returns the vectorizer object and the final matrix representation of the sentences. We will use the vectorizer object later on to encode new, unseen sentences. In *step 4*, we use the preceding two functions on the sherlock_holmes_1.txt file. In *step 5*, we print out the matrix that was created from encoding the input text.

The CountVectorizer object makes a representation of each document by looking at whether each word is in its vocabulary or all the words seen in all the documents are present in a particular document. This can be seen in the sparse representation, where each tuple is a pair, with the document number and word number and the corresponding number, which is the number of times the word appears in that particular document. For example, the sixth entry in the sparse matrix is as follows:

```
  (0, 0)              1
```

This means that there is one word with the number 0 in the document number 0. Document number 0 is the first sentence from our text: **To Sherlock Holmes she is always _the_ woman**. The word number 0 is the first word from the vocabulary listing, which is **_the_**. The ordering of words is alphabetical according to their appearance in the whole text. There is one word, **_the_**, in this sentence, and it is also the sixth word, corresponding to the sixth entry in the sparse matrix.

In *step 6*, we turn the sparse matrix into a dense one, where each sentence is represented with a vector. In *step 7*, we print the resulting matrix out, and we see that it is a nested list, where each individual list is a vector that represents each sentence in the text. In this form, the sentence representations are suitable to use in machine learning algorithms.

In *step 8*, we print out all the words that were used to create the vectorizer object. This list is sometimes needed to see which words are in the vocabulary, and which are not.

In *step 9*, we create a string variable with a new sentence that was not used to create the vectorizer object, and then apply the transformation to it. In *step 10*, we print out the sparse and dense matrices for this new sentence. It shows that three words from the vocabulary are present, which are **seen**, **of**, and **Holmes**. The other words were not present in the sentences the vectorizer was created on, and so they are absent from the new vectors.

There's more...

The CountVectorizer class contains several useful features, such as showing the results of a sentence analysis that shows only the words that are going to be used in the vector representation, excluding words that are very frequent, or excluding stopwords from an included list. We will explore these features here:

1. Import the CountVectorizer class and helper functions from *Chapter 1, Learning NLP Basics* :

    ```
    from sklearn.feature_extraction.text import
    CountVectorizer
    ```

    ```
    from Chapter01.dividing_into_sentences import read_text_
    file, preprocess_text, divide_into_sentences_nltk
    ```

2. Read in the text file, preprocess the text, and divide it into sentences:

    ```
    filename="sherlock_holmes_1.txt"
    ```

    ```
    sherlock_holmes_text = read_text_file(filename)
    ```

    ```
    sherlock_holmes_text = preprocess_text(sherlock_holmes_
    text)
    ```

    ```
    sentences = divide_into_sentences_nltk(sherlock_holmes_
    text)
    ```

3. Create a new vectorizer class. This time, use the stop_words argument:

    ```
    vectorizer = CountVectorizer(stop_words='english')
    ```

4. Use the vectorizer object to get the matrix:

    ```
    X = vectorizer.fit_transform(sentences)
    ```

5. We can print the vocabulary like so:

    ```
    print(vectorizer.get_feature_names())
    ```

6. The result will be a smaller set with very frequent words, such as **of, the, to**, and so on (stopwords), missing:

    ```
    ['_the_', 'abhorrent', 'actions', 'adjusted', 'adler',
    'admirable', 'admirably', 'admit', 'akin', 'balanced',
    'cold', 'crack', 'delicate', 'distracting', 'disturbing',
    'doubt', 'drawing', 'dubious', 'eclipses', 'emotion',
    'emotions', 'excellent', 'eyes', 'factor', 'false',
    'felt', 'finely', 'gibe', 'grit', 'heard', 'high',
    ```

```
'holmes', 'instrument', 'introduce', 'intrusions',
'irene', 'late', 'lenses', 'love', 'lover', 'machine',
'memory', 'men', 'mental', 'mention', 'mind', 'motives',
'nature', 'observer', 'observing', 'particularly',
'passions', 'perfect', 'placed', 'position', 'power',
'precise', 'predominates', 'questionable', 'reasoner',
'reasoning', 'results', 'save', 'seen', 'seldom',
'sensitive', 'sex', 'sherlock', 'sneer', 'softer',
'spoke', 'strong', 'temperament', 'things', 'throw',
'trained', 'veil', 'woman', 'world']
```

7. We can now apply the new vectorizer to one of the sentences in the original set and use the `build_analyzer` function to see the analysis of the sentence more clearly:

```
new_sentence = "And yet there was but one woman to him,
and that woman was the late Irene Adler, of dubious and
questionable memory."
new_sentence_vector = vectorizer.transform([new_
sentence])
analyze = vectorizer.build_analyzer()
print(analyze(new_sentence))
```

We can see that **and, yet, there, was, but, one, to, him, that, the**, and **of** are all missing from the printout of the sentence analysis:

```
['woman', 'woman', 'late', 'irene', 'adler', 'dubious',
'questionable', 'memory']
```

8. We can print out the sparse vector of the sentence like so:

```
print(new_sentence_vector)
```

9. The result will contain seven words:

(0, 4)	1
(0, 17)	1
(0, 35)	1
(0, 36)	1
(0, 41)	1
(0, 58)	1
(0, 77)	2

10. Instead of using a prebuilt stopwords list, we can limit the vocabulary by specifying either an absolute or relative maximum document frequency. We can specify this using the `max_df` argument, where we either provide it with an integer for the absolute document frequency or a float for the maximum percentage of documents. Our document set is very small, so it won't have an effect, but in a larger set, you would build the `CountVectorizer` object with a maximum document frequency, as follows:

```
vectorizer = CountVectorizer(max_df=0.8)
```

In this case, the vectorizer will consider words that appear in less than 80% of all documents.

Constructing the N-gram model

Representing a document as a bag of words is useful, but semantics is about more than just words in isolation. To capture word combinations, an n-gram model is useful. Its vocabulary consists not just of words, but word sequences, or n-grams. We will build a bigram model in this recipe, where bigrams are sequences of two words.

Getting ready

The `CountVectorizer` class is very versatile and allows us to construct n-gram models. We will use it again in this recipe. We will also explore how to build character n-gram models using this class.

How to do it...

Follow these steps:

1. Import the `CountVectorizer` class and helper functions from *Chapter 1, Learning NLP Basics*, from the *Putting documents into a bag of words* recipe:

```
from sklearn.feature_extraction.text import
CountVectorizer
from Chapter01.dividing_into_sentences import read_text_
file, preprocess_text, divide_into_sentences_nltk
from Chapter03.bag_of_words import get_sentences, get_
new_sentence_vector
```

2. Get the sentences from the `sherlock_holmes_1.txt` file:

```
sentences = get_sentences("sherlock_holmes_1.txt")
```

3. Create a new `vectorizer` class. In this case, we will use the `n_gram` argument:

```
bigram_vectorizer = CountVectorizer(ngram_range=(1, 2))
```

4. Use the `vectorizer` object to get the matrix:

```
X = bigram_vectorizer.fit_transform(sentences)
```

5. Print the result:

```
print(X)
```

6. The resulting matrix is a `scipy.sparse.csr.csr_matrix` object, and the beginning of its printout looks like this:

```
  (0, 269)      1
  (0, 229)      1
  (0, 118)      1
  (0, 226)      1
  (0, 136)      1
  (0, 20)       1
  (0, 0)        1
  (0, 299)      1
  (0, 275)      1
  (0, 230)      1
  (0, 119)      1
  (0, 228)      1
  ...
```

7. To get a `numpy.matrixlib.defmatrix.matrix` object, where each sentence is a vector, use the `todense()` function:

```
denseX = X.todense()
print(denseX)
```

8. The printout looks like this:

```
[[1 1 0 ... 0 0 0]
 [0 0 0 ... 0 0 0]
```

```
[0 0 0 ... 0 0 0]
```

```
...
```

```
[0 0 0 ... 0 0 0]
```

```
[0 0 0 ... 1 0 0]
```

```
[0 0 0 ... 0 1 1]]
```

9. Let's look at the vocabulary that the model uses:

```
print(bigram_vectorizer.get_feature_names())
```

The resulting vocabulary includes each word and each bigram:

```
['_the_', '_the_ woman', 'abhorrent', 'abhorrent
to', 'actions', 'adjusted', 'adjusted temperament',
'adler', 'adler of', 'admirable', 'admirable things',
'admirably', 'admirably balanced', 'admit', 'admit
such', 'akin', 'akin to', 'all', 'all emotions', 'all
his', 'always', 'always _the_', 'and', 'and actions',
'and finely', 'and observing', 'and predominates',
'and questionable', 'and sneer', 'and that', 'and yet',
'any', 'any emotion', 'any other', 'as', 'as his', 'as
lover', 'balanced', 'balanced mind', 'be', 'be more',
'but', 'but admirably', 'but as', 'but for', 'but one',
'cold', 'cold precise', 'crack', 'crack in', 'delicate',
'delicate and', 'distracting', 'distracting factor',
'disturbing', 'disturbing than', 'doubt', 'doubt upon',
'drawing', 'drawing the', 'dubious', 'dubious and',
'eclipses', 'eclipses and', 'emotion', 'emotion akin',
'emotion in', 'emotions', 'emotions and', 'excellent',
'excellent for', 'eyes', 'eyes she', 'factor', 'factor
which', 'false', 'false position', 'felt', 'felt any',
'finely', 'finely adjusted', 'for', 'for drawing', 'for
irene', 'for the', 'from', 'from men', 'gibe', 'gibe
and', 'grit', 'grit in', 'has', 'has seen', 'have', 'have
placed', 'have seldom', 'he', 'he felt', 'he never',
'he was', 'he would', 'heard', 'heard him', 'her', 'her
sex', 'her under', 'high', 'high power', 'him', 'him
and', 'him mention', 'himself', 'himself in', 'his', 'his
cold', 'his eyes', 'his mental', 'his own', 'holmes',
'holmes she', 'in', 'in false', 'in his', 'in nature',
'in one', 'in sensitive', 'instrument', 'instrument or',
'into', 'into his', 'introduce', 'introduce distracting',
'intrusions', 'intrusions into', 'irene', 'irene adler',
'is', 'is always', 'it', 'it the', 'it was', 'late',
'late irene', 'lenses', 'lenses would', 'love', 'love
```

```
for', 'lover', 'lover he', 'machine', 'machine that',
'memory', 'men', 'men motives', 'mental', 'mental
results', 'mention', 'mention her', 'might', 'might
throw', 'mind', 'more', 'more disturbing', …]
```

10. We can now also use the `CountVectorizer` object to represent new sentences that were not in the original document set. We will use the sentence *I had seen little of Holmes lately*, which is the next sentence after the excerpt in `sherlock_holmes_1.txt`. The `transform` function expects a list of documents, so we will create a new list where the sentence is the only element:

```
new_sentence = "I had seen little of Holmes lately."
new_sentence_vector = \
bigram_vectorizer.transform([new_sentence])
```

11. We can now print the sparse and dense representations of this new sentence:

```
print(new_sentence_vector)
print(new_sentence_vector.todense())
```

The result will be as follows:

```
  (0, 118)        1
  (0, 179)        1
  (0, 219)        1
[[0 0 0 0 0 0 0 0 0 0 0 0 0 0 0 0 0 0 0 0 0 0 0 0 0 0 0 0 0 0 0
 0 0 0 0 0 0 0 0
  0 0 0 0 0 0 0 0 0 0 0 0 0 0 0 0 0 0 0 0 0 0 0 0 0 0 0 0 0 0 0
 0 0 0 0 0 0 0 0
  0 0 0 0 0 0 0 0 0 0 0 0 0 0 0 0 0 0 0 0 0 0 0 0 0 0 0 0 0 0 0
 0 0 0 0 0 0 0 0
  0 0 0 0 0 0 0 0 0 0 1 0 0 0 0 0 0 0 0 0 0 0 0 0 0 0 0 0 0 0 0
 0 0 0 0 0 0 0 0
  0 0 0 0 0 0 0 0 0 0 0 0 0 0 0 0 0 0 0 0 0 0 0 0 0 0 0 0 0 0 0
 0 0 0 0 0 0 0 1
  0 0 0 0 0 0 0 0 0 0 0 0 0 0 0 0 0 0 0 0 0 0 0 0 0 0 0 0 0 0 0
 0 0 0 0 0 0 0 0
  0 0 0 1 0 0 0 0 0 0 0 0 0 0 0 0 0 0 0 0 0 0 0 0 0 0 0 0 0 0 0
 0 0 0 0 0 0 0 0
  0 0 0 0 0 0 0 0 0 0 0 0 0 0 0 0 0 0 0 0 0 0 0 0 0 0 0 0 0 0 0
 0 0 0 0 0 0 0 0
  0 0 0 0 0 0 0 0 0 0 0 0 0 0 0 0 0 0 0 0 0 0]]
```

12. Let's compare the preceding representation with the representation of a sentence from the original input text; that is, *And yet there was but one woman to him, and that woman was the late Irene Adler, of dubious and questionable memory*:

```
new_sentence1 = " And yet there was but one woman to him,
and that woman was the late Irene Adler, of dubious and
questionable memory."
```

```
new_sentence_vector1 = vectorizer.transform([new_
sentence])
```

13. We will print the sparse and dense representations of this sentence:

```
print(new_sentence_vector1)
```

```
print(new_sentence_vector1.todense())
```

14. The result will be as follows:

```
(0, 7)              1
(0, 8)              1
(0, 22)             3
(0, 27)             1
(0, 29)             1
...
[[0 0 0 0 0 0 0 1 1 0 0 0 0 0 0 0 0 0 0 0 0 0 3 0 0 0 0 1
0 1 1 0 0 0 0 0
 0 0 0 0 0 1 0 0 0 1 0 0 0 0 0 0 0 0 0 0 0 0 0 0 1 1 0 0
0 0 0 0 0 0 0 0
 0 0 0 0 0 0 0 0 0 0 0 0 0 0 0 0 0 0 0 0 0 0 0 0 0 0 0 0
0 0 0 0 0 0 0 0
 1 1 0 0 0 0 0 0 0 0 0 0 0 0 0 0 0 0 0 0 0 0 0 0 0 0 1 1
0 0 0 0 0 1 1 0
 0 0 0 0 0 0 0 1 0 0 0 0 0 0 0 0 0 0 0 0 0 0 0 0 0 0 0 0
0 0 0 0 0 0 0 1
 1 0 0 0 1 0 0 1 0 0 0 0 0 0 0 0 0 0 0 0 0 0 0 0 0 0 0 0
0 0 1 1 0 0 0 0
 0 0 0 0 0 0 0 0 0 0 0 0 0 0 0 0 0 0 0 0 0 0 0 0 0 0 0 0
0 0 0 1 0 0 0 1
 1 1 0 0 0 0 0 0 0 1 1 0 0 0 0 0 0 1 0 1 0 0 0 0 0 0 0 0
0 0 0 0 2 1 0 0
 1 0 0 0 0 0 0 0 0 0 0 2 1 1 0 0 0 0 0 1 1]]
```

How it works...

In *step 1*, we import the necessary objects and functions, and in *step 2*, we create a list of sentences from the `sherlock_holmes_1.txt` file. In *step 3*, we create a new `CountVectorizer` object that has an extra argument, `ngram_range`. The `CountVectorizer` class, when the `ngram_range` argument is set, counts not only individual words, but also word combinations, where the number of words in the combinations depends on the numbers provided to the `ngram_range` argument. We provided `ngram_range=(1,2)` as the argument, which means that the number of words in the combinations ranges from 1 to 2, so unigrams and bigrams are counted.

In *step 4*, we use the `bigram_vectorizer` object and create the matrix, and in *step 5*, we print the matrix. The result looks very similar to the matrix output shown in the *Putting documents into a bag of words* recipe, with the only difference that the output should now be longer as it includes not just individual words, but also bigrams, or sequences of two words.

In *step 6*, we create a dense matrix and print it out. In *step 7*, we print out the vocabulary of the vectorizer and we see that it includes both individual words and bigrams.

In *step 8*, we transform an unseen sentence using the vectorizer and in *step 9*, we print out both the sparse and dense vectors for the sentence. In *step 10*, we transform a sentence that was part of the original text and in *step 11*, we print out its sparse and dense representations. Once we analyze the new sentence, we see that only three words (or bigrams) from the vectorizer's original vocabulary are present in the sentence, while the sentence that was part of the original dataset has a lot more words counted. This shows how sentences that are very different from the original sentence set the vectorizer was fitted on will be poorly represented, since most of the words and word combinations will be missing from the vectorizer's vocabulary.

There's more...

We can use trigrams, quadrigrams, and more in the vectorizer by providing the corresponding tuple to the `ngram_range` argument. The downside of this is the ever-expanding vocabulary and the growth of sentence vectors, since each sentence vector has to have an entry for each word in the input vocabulary.

Representing texts with TF-IDF

We can go one step further and use the TF-IDF algorithm to count words and ngrams in incoming documents. **TF-IDF** stands for **term frequency-inverse document frequency** and gives more weight to words that are unique to a document than to words that are frequent, but repeated throughout most documents. This allows us to give more weight to words uniquely characteristic to particular documents. You can find out more at `https://scikit-learn.org/stable/modules/feature_extraction.html#tfidf-term-weighting`.

In this recipe, we will use a different type of vectorizer that can apply the TF-IDF algorithm to the input text. Like the `CountVectorizer` class, it has an analyzer that we will use to show the representations of new sentences.

Getting ready

We will be using the `TfidfVectorizer` class from the `sklearn` package. We will also be using the stopwords list from *Chapter 1, Learning NLP Basics*.

How to do it...

The `TfidfVectorizer` class allows for all the functionality of `CountVectorizer`, except that it uses the TF-IDF algorithm to count the words instead of direct counts. The other features of the class should be familiar. We will again be using the `sherlock_holmes_1.txt` file.

Here are the steps you should follow to build and use the TF-IDF vectorizer:

1. Import the `TfidfVectorizer` class, `nltk`, and the relevant helper functions:

```
import nltk
import string
from sklearn.feature_extraction.text import
TfidfVectorizer
from nltk.stem.snowball import SnowballStemmer
from Chapter01.removing_stopwords import read_in_csv
from Chapter03.bag_of_words import get_sentences
```

2. Define the stemmer and the stopwords file path:

```
stemmer = SnowballStemmer('english')
stopwords_file_path = "Chapter01/stopwords.csv"
```

3. Get the sentences from the `sherlock_holmes_1.txt` file:

```
sentences = get_sentences("sherlock_holmes_1.txt")
```

4. We will use a function to tokenize and stem every word, including stopwords. See the *Dividing sentences into words* and *Word stemming* recipes in *Chapter 1, Learning NLP Basics*, for more information:

```
def tokenize_and_stem(sentence):
    tokens = nltk.word_tokenize(sentence)
    filtered_tokens = [t for t in tokens if t not in \
                        string.punctuation]
    stems = [stemmer.stem(t) for t in filtered_tokens]
    return stems
```

5. Read in, tokenize, and stem the stopwords:

```
stopword_list = read_in_csv(stopwords_file_path)
stemmed_stopwords = [tokenize_and_stem(stopword)[0] for \
                     stopword in stopword_list]
stopword_list = stopword_list + stemmed_stopwords
```

6. Create a new vectorizer class and fit the incoming sentences. You might see some warnings here, which is fine:

```
tfidf_vectorizer = \
TfidfVectorizer(max_df=0.90, max_features=200000,
                min_df=0.05, stop_words=stopword_list,
                use_idf=True,tokenizer=tokenize_and_stem,
                ngram_range=(1,3))
tfidf_vectorizer = tfidf_vectorizer.fit(sentences)
```

7. Use the `vectorizer` object to get the matrix:

```
tfidf_matrix = tfidf_vectorizer.transform(sentences)
```

8. Print the result:

```
print(tfidf_matrix)
```

9. The resulting matrix is a `scipy.sparse.csr.csr_matrix` object, and the beginning of its printout looks like this:

(0, 195)	0.2892833606818738
(0, 167)	0.33843668854613723
(0, 166)	0.33843668854613723
(0, 165)	0.33843668854613723
(0, 84)	0.33843668854613723
(0, 83)	0.33843668854613723
(0, 82)	0.33843668854613723
(0, 1)	0.33843668854613723
(0, 0)	0.33843668854613723
...	

10. To get a `numpy.matrixlib.defmatrix.matrix` object, where each sentence is a vector, use the `todense()` function:

```
dense_matrix = tfidf_matrix.todense()
```

Its printout looks like this:

```
[[0.33843669 0.33843669 0.        ... 0.         0.
0.        ]
 [0.         0.         0.        ... 0.         0.
0.        ]
 [0.         0.         0.        ... 0.         0.
0.        ]
 ...
 [0.         0.         0.        ... 0.         0.
0.        ]
 [0.         0.         0.        ... 0.         0.
0.        ]
 [0.         0.         0.        ... 0.         0.
0.        ]] [0 0 0 ... 1 0 0]
 [0 0 0 ... 0 1 1]]
```

11. Let's look at the vocabulary that the model uses:

```
print(tfidf_vectorizer.get_feature_names())
```

The resulting vocabulary includes each stemmed word, each bigram, and each trigram:

```
[['_the_', '_the_ woman', 'abhorr', 'abhorr cold',
'abhorr cold precis', 'action', 'adjust', 'adjust
tempera', 'adjust tempera introduc', 'adler', 'adler
dubious', 'adler dubious question', 'admir', 'admir
balanc', 'admir balanc mind', 'admir observer—excel',
'admir observer—excel draw', 'admit', 'admit intrus',
'admit intrus own', 'akin', 'akin love', 'akin love
iren', 'balanc', 'balanc mind', 'cold', 'cold precis',
'cold precis admir', 'crack', 'crack own', 'crack own
high-pow', 'delic', 'delic fine', 'delic fine adjust',
'distract', 'distract factor', 'distract factor throw',
'disturb', 'disturb strong', 'disturb strong emot',
'doubt', 'doubt mental', 'doubt mental result', 'draw',
'draw veil', 'draw veil men', 'dubious', 'dubious
question', 'dubious question memori', 'eclips', 'eclips
predomin', 'eclips predomin whole', 'emot', 'emot
abhorr', 'emot abhorr cold', 'emot akin', 'emot akin
love', 'emot natur', 'eye', 'eye eclips', 'eye eclips
predomin', 'factor', 'factor throw', 'factor throw
doubt', 'fals', 'fals posit', 'felt', 'felt emot', 'felt
emot akin', 'fine', 'fine adjust', 'fine adjust tempera',
'gibe', 'gibe sneer', 'grit', 'grit sensit', 'grit sensit
instrument', 'heard', 'heard mention', 'high-pow', 'high-
pow lens', 'high-pow lens disturb', 'holm', 'holm _the_',
'holm _the_ woman', 'instrument', 'instrument crack',
'instrument crack own', 'introduc', 'introduc distract',
'introduc distract factor', 'intrus', 'intrus own',
'intrus own delic', 'iren', 'iren adler', 'iren adler
dubious', 'lens', 'lens disturb', 'lens disturb strong',
…]
```

12. Let's build an analyzer function and analyze the sentence *To Sherlock Holmes she is always _the_ woman*:

```
analyze = tfidf_vectorizer.build_analyzer()
print(analyze("To Sherlock Holmes she is always _the_
woman."))
```

This is the result:

```
['sherlock', 'holm', '_the_', 'woman', 'sherlock holm',
'holm _the_', '_the_ woman', 'sherlock holm _the_', 'holm
_the_ woman']
```

How it works...

The `TfidfVectorizer` class works almost exactly like the `CountVectorizer` class, differing only in the way the word frequencies are calculated, so most of the steps should be familiar here. Word frequencies are calculated as follows. For each word, the overall frequency is a product of the term frequency and the inverse document frequency. Term frequency is the number of times the word occurs in the document. Inverse document frequency is the total number of documents divided by the number of documents where the word occurs. Usually, these frequencies are logarithmically scaled.

In *step 1*, we import the `TfidfVectorizer` and `SnowballStemmer` classes and helper functions. In *step 2*, we define the stemmer object and the path to the stopwords file. In *step 3*, we create the list of sentences from the `sherlock_holmes_1.txt` file.

In *step 4*, we define the `tokenize_and_stem` function, which we will use to tokenize and stem the words in a sentence.

In *step 5*, we read in the stopwords list and apply the `tokenize_and_stem` function to it. Since we will be stemming the words in the text, we also need to stem the stopwords. The reason we need to do this is because if we leave the stopwords unstemmed, the stemmed words in the dataset will not match them. The functions also exclude all punctuation from text since we do not want to include n-grams with punctuation in them. To do that, we check if each token is included in the `string.punctuation` set, which lists all punctuation symbols. In *step 6*, we create a new vectorizer class and then fit the sentences. The `min_df` and `max_df` arguments limit the minimum and maximum document frequency, respectively. If the corpus is large enough, the maximum document frequency can take care of the stopwords by excluding words that are very frequent across the documents. For our small corpus, I had to provide the stopword list. The `min_df` and `max_df` arguments are either floats between 0 and 1, representing a proportion of documents, or an integer, representing an absolute count. The `max_features` argument caps the number of words and n-grams in the vocabulary at the number provided. For more information about `TfidfVectorizer`, see `https://scikit-learn.org/stable/modules/generated/sklearn.feature_extraction.text.TfidfVectorizer.html`.

In *step 7*, we use the vectorizer to get the matrix encoding the sentences and in *step 8*, we print the result. We can see that the resulting matrix is very similar to the matrices in the *Putting documents into a bag of words* and *Constructing the N-gram model* recipes of this chapter. The difference is that the frequency count is a fraction, since it is a product of two ratios.

In *step 9*, we create a dense matrix that represents each sentence as a vector.

In *step 10*, we print out the vocabulary of the vectorizer, which includes unigrams as well as bigrams.

In *step 11*, we create the analyzer object and analyze a sentence from the `sherlock_holmes_1.txt` file. The result shows that now, the sentence is represented with uni-, bi- and trigrams, along with words that have been stemmed and whose stopwords have been removed.

There's more...

We can build `TfidfVectorizer` and use character n-grams instead of word n-grams. Character n-grams use the character, and not the word, as their basic unit. For example, if we were to build character n-grams for the phrase *the woman* with the n-gram range (1, 3), its set would be [t, h, e, w, o, m, a, n, th, he, wo, om, ma, an, the, wom, oma, man]. In many experimental settings, models based on character n-grams perform better than word-based n-gram models.

We will use the same Sherlock Holmes text file, `sherlock_holmes_1.txt`, and the same class, `TfidfVectorizer`. We will not need a tokenizer function or a stopwords list, since the unit of analysis is the character and not the word. The steps to create the vectorizer and analyze a sentence are as follows:

1. Get the sentences from the `sherlock_holmes_1.txt` file:

```
sentences = get_sentences("sherlock_holmes_1.txt")
```

2. Create a new `vectorizer` class and fit the incoming sentences:

```
tfidf_char_vectorizer = \
TfidfVectorizer(analyzer='char_wb',
                max_df=0.90,
                max_features=200000,
                min_df=0.05,
                use_idf=True,
                ngram_range=(1,3))
tfidf_char_vectorizer = tfidf_char_vectorizer.
fit(sentences)
```

3. Use the `vectorizer` object to get the matrix:

```
tfidf_matrix = tfidf_char_vectorizer.transform(sentences)
```

4. Print the result:

```
print(tfidf_matrix)
```

Predictably, the resulting matrix is much larger than the ones based on words. The beginning of its printout looks like this:

(0, 763)	0.12662434631923655
(0, 762)	0.12662434631923655
(0, 753)	0.05840470946313
(0, 745)	0.10823388151187574
(0, 744)	0.0850646359499111
(0, 733)	0.12662434631923655
(0, 731)	0.07679517427049085
(0, 684)	0.07679517427049085
(0, 683)	0.07679517427049085
(0, 675)	0.05840470946313
(0, 639)	0.21646776302375148
(0, 638)	0.21646776302375148
...	

5. To get a `numpy.matrixlib.defmatrix.matrix` object, where each sentence is a vector, use the `todense()` function:

```
dense_matrix = tfidf_matrix.todense()
```

Its printout looks like this:

```
[[0.12662435 0.12662435 0.          ... 0.          0.
  0.          ]
 [0.          0.          0.          ... 0.          0.
  0.          ]
 [0.          0.          0.          ... 0.          0.
  0.          ]
 ...
 [0.          0.          0.07119069 ... 0.          0.
  0.          ]
 [0.          0.          0.17252729 ... 0.          0.
  0.          ]
```

```
  [0.        0.        0.       ... 0.        0.
  0.        ]]
```

6. Let's look at the vocabulary that the model uses:

```
print(tfidf_char_vectorizer.get_feature_names())
```

The resulting vocabulary includes each character, as well as the character bigrams and trigrams. The beginning of the printout looks like this:

```
[' _', ' _t', ' a ', ' ab', ' ac', ' ad', ' ak', ' al',
' an', ' as', ' b', ' ba', ' be', ' bu', ' c', ' co',
' cr', ' d', ' de', ' di', ' do', ' dr', ' du', ' e',
' ec', ' em', ' ey', ' f', ' fa', ' fe', ' fi', ' fo',
' fr', ' g', ' gi', ' gr', ' ha', ' he', ' hi', ' ho',
' i', ' i ', ' in', ' ir', ' is', ' it', ' l', ' la',
' le', ' lo', ' m', ' ma', ' me', ' mi', ' mo', ' n',
' na', ' ne', ' no', ' o', ' ob', ' of', ' on', ' or',
' ot', ' ow', ' p', ' pa', ' pe', ' pl', ' po', ' pr',
' q', ' qu', ' r', ' re', ' s', ' sa', ' se', ' sh', '
sn', ' so', ' sp', ' st', ' su', ' ta', ' te', ' th', '
to', ' tr', ' u', ' un', ' up', ' v', ' ve', ' wa', '
we', ' wh', ' wi', ' wo', ' y', ' ye', ',', ', ', '-',
'-p', '-po', '_', '_ ', '_t', '_th', 'a ', 'ab', 'abh',
'abl', 'ac', 'ace', 'ach', 'ack', 'act', 'ad', 'adj',
'adl', 'adm', 'ai', 'ain', 'ak', 'ake', 'aki', 'al', 'al
', 'ala', 'all', 'als', 'alw', 'am', 'ame', 'an ', 'an.',
'anc', 'and', 'any', 'ar', 'ard', 'arl', 'art', 'as', 'as
', 'as,', 'aso', 'ass', 'at', 'at ', 'ate', 'atu', 'av',
'ave', 'aw', 'awi', 'ay', 'ays', 'b', 'ba', 'bal', 'be',
'be ', 'bh', 'bho', 'bi', 'bin', 'bio', 'bl', 'ble',
'bly', 'bs', 'bse', 'bt', 'bt ', 'bu', 'but', 'c', 'ca',
'cat', 'ce', 'ce ', 'ced', 'cel', 'ch', 'ch ', 'chi',
'ci', 'cis', 'ck', 'ck ', 'cl', 'cli', 'co', 'col', 'cr',
'cra', 'ct', 'ct ', 'cti', 'cto', 'cu', 'cul', …]
```

7. Let's build an analyzer function and analyze the sentence *To Sherlock Holmes she is always _the_ woman*:

```
analyze = tfidf_char_vectorizer.build_analyzer()
print(analyze("To Sherlock Holmes she is always _the_
woman."))
```

This is the result:

```
[' ', 't', 'o', ' ', ' t', 'to', 'o ', ' to', 'to ', ' ',
's', 'h', 'e', 'r', 'l', 'o', 'c', 'k', ' ', ' s', 'sh',
'he', 'er', 'rl', 'lo', 'oc', 'ck', 'k ', ' sh', 'she',
'her', 'erl', 'rlo', 'loc', 'ock', 'ck ', ' ', 'h', 'o',
'l', 'm', 'e', 's', ' ', ' h', 'ho', 'ol', 'lm', 'me',
'es', 's ', ' ho', 'hol', 'olm', 'lme', 'mes', 'es ', '
', 's', 'h', 'e', ' ', ' s', 'sh', 'he', 'e ', ' sh',
'she', 'he ', ' ', 'i', 's', ' ', ' i', 'is', 's ', '
is', 'is ', ' ', 'a', 'l', 'w', 'a', 'y', 's', ' ', ' a',
'al', 'lw', 'wa', 'ay', 'ys', 's ', ' al', 'alw', 'lwa',
'way', 'ays', 'ys ', ' ', '_', 't', 'h', 'e', '_', ' ',
' _', '_t', 'th', 'he', 'e_', '_ ', ' _t', '_th', 'the',
'he_', 'e_ ', ' ', 'w', 'o', 'm', 'a', 'n', '.', ' ', '
w', 'wo', 'om', 'ma', 'an', 'n.', '. ', ' wo', 'wom',
'oma', 'man', 'an.', 'n. ']
```

Using word embeddings

In this recipe we switch gears and learn how to represent *words* using word embeddings, which are powerful because they are a result of training a neural network that predicts a word from all other words in the sentence. The resulting vector embeddings are similar for words that occur in similar contexts. We will use the embeddings to show these similarities.

Getting ready

In this recipe, we will use a pretrained word2vec model, which can be found at http://vectors.nlpl.eu/repository/20/40.zip. Download the model and unzip it in the Chapter03 directory. You should now have a file whose path is .../Chapter03/40/model.bin.

We will also be using the gensim package to load and use the model. Install it using pip:

```
pip install gensim
```

How to do it...

We will load the model, demonstrate some features of the `gensim` package, and then compute a sentence vector using the word embeddings. Let's get started:

1. Import the `KeyedVectors` object from `gensim.models` and `numpy`:

    ```
    from gensim.models import KeyedVectors
    import numpy as np
    ```

2. Assign the model path to a variable:

    ```
    w2vec_model_path = "Chapter03/40/model.bin"
    ```

3. Load the pretrained model:

    ```
    model = KeyedVectors.load_word2vec_format(w2vec_model_
    path,

                                    binary=True)
    ```

4. Using the pretrained model, we can now load individual word vectors:

    ```
    print(model['holmes'])
    ```

5. The result will be as follows:

    ```
    [-0.309647 -0.127936 -0.136244 -0.252969  0.410695
    0.206325   0.119236

      -0.244745 -0.436801  0.058889  0.237439  0.247656
    0.072103   0.044183

      -0.424878  0.367344  0.153287  0.343856  0.232269
    -0.181432 -0.050021

       0.225756  0.71465  -0.564166 -0.168468 -0.153668
    0.300445 -0.220122

      -0.021261  0.25779  ...]
    ```

6. We can also get words that are most similar to a given word. For example, let's print out the words most similar to *Holmes* (lowercase, since all the words are lowercased in the training process):

    ```
    print(model.most_similar(['holmes'], topn=15))
    ```

The result is as follows:

```
[('sherlock', 0.8416914939880371), ('parker',
0.8099909424781799), ('moriarty', 0.8039606809616089),
('sawyer', 0.8002701997756958), ('moore',
0.7932805418968201), ('wolfe', 0.7923581600189209),
('hale', 0.791009247303009), ('doyle',
0.7906038761138916), ('holmes.the', 0.7895270586013794),
('watson', 0.7887690663337708), ('yates',
0.7882785797119141), ('stevenson', 0.7879440188407898),
('spencer', 0.7877693772315979), ('goodwin',
0.7866846919059753), ('baxter', 0.7864187955856323)]
```

7. We can now also compute a sentence vector by averaging all the word vectors in the sentence. We will use the sentence It *was not that he felt any emotion akin to love for Irene Adler*:

```
sentence = "It was not that he felt any emotion akin to
love for Irene Adler."
```

8. Let's define a function that will take a sentence and a model and will return a list of the sentence word vectors:

```
def get_word_vectors(sentence, model):
    word_vectors = []
    for word in sentence:
        try:
            word_vector = model.get_vector(word.lower())
            word_vectors.append(word_vector)
        except KeyError:
            continue
    return word_vectors
```

9. Now, let's define a function that will take the word vector list and compute the sentence vector:

```
def get_sentence_vector(word_vectors):
    matrix = np.array(word_vectors)
    centroid = np.mean(matrix[:,:], axis=0)
    return centroid
```

> **Important Note**
>
> Averaging the word vectors to get the sentence vector is only one way of
> approaching this task, and is not without its problems. One alternative is to
> train a doc2vec model, where sentences, paragraphs, and whole documents can
> all be units instead of words.

10. We can now compute the sentence vector:

```
word_vectors = get_word_vectors(sentence, model)
sentence_vector = get_sentence_vector(word_vectors)
print(sentence_vector)
```

11. The result is as follows:

```
[ 0.09226871  0.14478634  0.23788658 -0.31754282
0.42911175 -0.05198449

   0.12572111  0.01170996 -0.01138579  0.05200932
0.15247145  0.34026343

   0.12961692  0.05010585 -0.09165132  0.3782767
0.08390289  0.30078036

  -0.24396846  0.42507184 -0.13556597  0.157348
0.19739327 -0.13114193

  -0.16301586  0.19061208 ...]
```

How it works...

In *step 1*, we import the necessary objects. In *step 2*, we assign the path of the model we
downloaded in the *Getting ready* section to the w2vec_model_path variable. In *step 3*,
we load the model.

In *step 4*, we load the word vector for the word *Holmes*. We have to lowercase it since all
the words in the model are in lowercase. The result is a long vector that represents this
word in the word2vec model.

In *step 5*, we get 15 words that are most similar to the input word. The output prints out
the words that are the most similar (occur in similar contexts), as well as their similarity
scores. The score is the cosine distance between a pair of vectors, in this case representing
a pair of words. The larger the score, the more similar the two words. In this case, the
result is pretty good, as it contains the words *Sherlock*, *Moriarty*, *Watson*, and *Doyle*.

In the next few steps, we compute a sentence vector by averaging the word vectors. This is one approach to representing sentences using word2vec, and it has its disadvantages. One of the challenges of this approach is representing words that are not present in the model.

In *step 6*, we initialize the `sentence` variable with a sentence from the text. In *step 7*, we create the `get_word_vectors` function, which returns a list of all word vectors in the sentence. The function reads the word vector from the model and appends it to the `word_vectors` list. It also catches the `KeyError` error that is raised if the word is not present in the model.

In *step 8*, we create the `get_sentence_vector` function, which takes in a list of words vectors and returns their average. In order to compute the average, we represent the matrix as a NumPy array and use NumPy's `mean` function to get the average vector.

In *step 9*, we compute the word vectors for the sentence we defined in *step 6*, and then the sentence vector using the functions we just defined in *steps 7* and *8*. We then print the resulting sentence vector.

There's more...

There are some other fun things `gensim` can do with a pretrained model. For example, it can find a word that doesn't match from a list of words and find a word that is most similar to the given word from a list. Let's look at these:

1. Import the `KeyedVectors` object from `gensim.models`:

    ```
    from gensim.models import KeyedVectors
    ```

2. Assign the model path to a variable:

    ```
    w2vec_model_path = "Chapter03/40/model.bin"
    ```

3. Load the pretrained model:

    ```
    model = \
    KeyedVectors.load_word2vec_format(w2vec_model_path,
                                        binary=True)
    ```

4. Compile a list of words with one that doesn't match:

    ```
    words = ['banana', 'apple', 'computer', 'strawberry']
    ```

5. Apply the `doesnt_match` function to the list and print the result:

    ```
    print(model.doesnt_match(words))
    ```

The result will be as follows:

```
computer
```

6. Now, let's find a word that's most similar to another word:

```
word = "cup"
words = ['glass', 'computer', 'pencil', 'watch']
print(model.most_similar_to_given(word, words))
```

The result will be as follows:

```
glass
```

See also

There are many other pretrained models available, including in other languages; see `http://vectors.nlpl.eu/repository/` for more details.

Some of the pretrained models include part of speech information, which can be helpful when you're disambiguating words. These models concatenate words with their **part-of-speech (POS)**, such as cat_NOUN, so keep that in mind when using them.

To learn more about the theory behind word2vec, you could start here: `https://jalammar.github.io/illustrated-word2vec/`.

Training your own embeddings model

We can now train our own word2vec model on a corpus. For this task, we will use the top 20 Project Guttenberg books, which includes *The Adventures of Sherlock Holmes*. The reason for this is that training a model on just one book will result in suboptimal results. Once we get more text, the results will be better.

Getting ready

You can download the dataset for this recipe from Kaggle: `https://www.kaggle.com/currie32/project-gutenbergs-top-20-books`. The dataset includes files in RTF format, so you will have to save them as text. We will use the same package, `gensim`, to train our custom model.

We will use the `pickle` package to save the model on disk. If you do not have it installed, install it by using pip:

```
pip install pickle
```

How to do it...

We will read in all 20 books and use the text to create a `word2vec` model. Make sure all the books are located in one directory. Let's get started:

1. Import the necessary packages and functions:

```
import gensim
import pickle
from os import listdir
from os.path import isfile, join
from Chapter03.bag_of_words import get_sentences
from Chapter01.tokenization import tokenize_nltk
```

2. Assign the path of the `books` directory and the model path (where the model will be saved) to variables:

```
word2vec_model_path = "word2vec.model"
books_dir = "1025_1853_bundle_archive"
```

3. The `get_all_book_sentences` function will read all the text files from a directory and return a list containing all the sentences from them:

```
def get_all_book_sentences(directory):
    text_files = \
    [join(directory, f) for f in listdir(directory) if \
      isfile(join(directory, f)) and ".txt" in f]
    all_sentences = []
    for text_file in text_files:
        sentences = get_sentences(text_file)
        all_sentences = all_sentences + sentences
    return all_sentences
```

4. The `train_word2vec` function will train the model and save it to a file using `pickle`:

```
def train_word2vec(words, word2vec_model_path):
    model = gensim.models.Word2Vec(words, window=5,
                                   size=200)
    model.train(words, total_examples=len(words),
                epochs=200)
```

```
pickle.dump(model, open(word2vec_model_path, 'wb'))
return model
```

5. Get the books directory's sentences:

```
sentences = get_all_book_sentences(books_dir)
```

6. Tokenize and lowercase all the sentences:

```
sentences = [tokenize_nltk(s.lower()) for s in sentences]
```

7. Train the model. This step will take several minutes to run:

```
model = train_word2vec(sentences, word2vec_model_path)
```

8. We can now see which most similar words the model returns for different input words, such as *river*:

```
w1 = "river"
words = model.wv.most_similar(w1, topn=10)
print(words)
```

Every time a model is trained, the results will be different. My results look like this:

```
[('shore', 0.5025173425674438), ('woods',
0.46839720010757446), ('raft', 0.44671306014060974),
('illinois', 0.44637370109558105), ('hill',
0.4400100111961365), ('island', 0.43077412247657776),
('rock', 0.4293714761734009), ('stream',
0.42731013894081116), ('strand', 0.42297834157943726),
('road', 0.4181318283081 0547)]
```

How it works...

The code trains a neural network that predicts a word when given a sentence with words blanked out. The byproduct of the neural network being trained is a vector representation for each word in the training vocabulary.

In *step 1*, we import the necessary functions and classes. In *step 2*, we initialize the directory and model variables. The directory should contain the books we are going to train the model on, while the model path should be where the model will be saved.

In *step 3*, we create the `get_all_book_sentences` function, which will return all the sentences in all the books in the dataset. The first line in this function creates a list of all text files in the given directory. Next, we have a loop where we get the sentences for each of the text files and add them to the `all_sentences` array, which we return at the end.

In *step 4*, we create the function that will train the word2vec model. The only required argument is the list of words, though some of the other important ones are `min_count`, `size`, `window`, and `workers`. `min_count` is the minimum number of times a word has to occur in the training corpus, with the default being 5. The `size` parameter sets the size of the word vector. `window` restricts the maximum number of words between the predicted and current word in a sentence. `workers` is the number of working threads; the more there are, the quicker the training will proceed. When training the model, the `epoch` parameter will determine the number of training iterations the model will go through.

At the end of the function, we save the model to the provided path.

In *step 6*, we get all the sentences from the books using the previously defined function. In *step 7*, we lowercase and tokenize them into words. Then, we train the word2vec model using the `train_word2vec` function; this will take several minutes. In *step 8*, we print out the words that are the most similar to the word *river* using the newly trained model. Since the model is different every time you train it, your results will be different from mine, but the resulting words should still be similar to *river* in the sense that they will be about nature.

There's more...

There are tools we can use to evaluate a `word2vec` model, although its creation is unsupervised. `gensim` comes with a file that lists word analogies, such as *Athens* to *Greece* being the same as *Moscow* to *Russia*. The `evaluate_word_analogies` function runs the analogies through the model and calculates how many were correct.

Here is how we can do this:

1. Import the necessary packages and functions:

    ```
    from gensim.test.utils import datapath
    from gensim.models import KeyedVectors
    import pickle
    ```

2. Load the previously pickled model:

    ```
    model = pickle.load(open(word2vec_model_path, 'rb'))
    ```

3. Evaluate the model against the provided file. This file is available in this book's GitHub repository at Chapter03/questions-words.txt:

```
(analogy_score, word_list) = \
model.wv.evaluate_word_analogies(datapath('questions-
words.txt'))
```

4. The score is the ratio of correct analogies, so a score of 1 would mean that all the analogies were correctly answered using the model, while a score of 0 means that none were. The word list is a detailed breakdown by word analogy. We can print the analogy score like so:

```
print(analogy_score)
```

The result will be as follows:

```
0.20059045432179762
```

5. We can now load the pretrained model and compare its performance to the 20-book model. These commands might take a few minutes to run:

```
pretrained_model_path = "Chapter03/40/model.bin"
pretrained_model = \
KeyedVectors.load_word2vec_format(pretrained_model_path,
                                  binary=True)
(analogy_score, word_list) = \
pretrained_model.evaluate_word_
analogies(datapath('questions-words.txt'))
print(analogy_score)
```

The result will be as follows:

```
0.5867802524889665
```

The pretrained model was trained on a much larger corpus, and, predictably, performs better. However, it still doesn't get a very high score. Your evaluation should be based on the type of text you are going to be working with, since the file that's provided with the gensim package is a generic evaluation.

> **Important Note**
> Make sure your evaluation is based on the type of data that you are going to be using in your application; otherwise, you risk having misleading evaluation results.

See also

There is an additional way of evaluating the model's performance; that is, by comparing the similarity between word pairs that have been assigned by the model to the human-assigned judgments. You can do this by using the `evaluate_word_pairs` function and the provided `wordsim353.tsv` data file. You can find out more at `https://radimrehurek.com/gensim/models/keyedvectors.html#gensim.models.keyedvectors.FastTextKeyedVectors.evaluate_word_pairs`.

Representing phrases – phrase2vec

Encoding words is useful, but usually, we deal with more complex units, such as phrases and sentences. Phrases are important because they specify more detail than just words. For example, the phrase *delicious fried rice* is very different than just the word *rice*.

In this recipe, we will train a `word2vec` model that uses phrases as well as words.

Getting ready

We will be using the Yelp restaurant review dataset in this recipe, which is available here: `https://www.yelp.com/dataset` (the file is about 4 GB.) Download the file and unzip it in the `Chapter03` folder. I downloaded the dataset in September 2020, and the results in the recipe are from that download. Your results might differ, since the dataset is updated by Yelp periodically.

The dataset is multilingual, and we will be working with the English reviews. In order to filter them, we will need the `langdetect` package. Install it using `pip`:

```
pip install langdetect
```

How to do it...

Our recipe will consist of two parts. The first part will discover phrases and tag them in the corpus, while the second part will train a `word2vec` model, following the same steps from the previous recipe. This recipe was inspired by reading Kavita Ganesan's work (`https://kavita-ganesan.com/how-to-incorporate-phrases-into-word2vec-a-text-mining-approach/`), and the idea of using stopwords as boundaries from phrases has been taken from there. Let's get started:

1. Import the necessary packages and functions:

    ```
    import nltk
    import string
    ```

```
import csv
import json
import pandas as pd
import gensim
from langdetect import detect
import pickle
from nltk import FreqDist
from Chapter01.dividing_into_sentences import \
divide_into_sentences_nltk
from Chapter01.tokenization import tokenize_nltk
from Chapter01.removing_stopwords import read_in_csv
```

2. Assign the path of the Yelp! reviews JSON file, the stopwords path, and read in the stopwords:

```
stopwords_file = "Chapter01/stopwords.csv"
stopwords = read_in_csv(stopwords_file)
yelp_reviews_file = "Chapter03/yelp-dataset/review.json"
```

3. The get_yelp_reviews function will read the first 10,000 lines from the file and only filter out English text:

```
def get_yelp_reviews(filename):
    reader = pd.read_json(filename, orient="records",
                          lines=True,
                          chunksize=10000)
    chunk = next(reader)
    text = ''
    for index, row in chunk.iterrows():
        row_text =row['text']
        lang = detect(row_text)
        if (lang == "en"):
            text = text + row_text.lower()
    return text
```

4. The `get_phrases` function records all the phrases that have been found in the text, and then creates a dictionary with the original phrase as the key and the phrases with underscores instead of spaces as the entry. The boundaries are stopwords or punctuation. Using this function, we will get all the phrases in the text and then annotate them in the dataset:

```python
def get_phrases(text):
    words = nltk.tokenize.word_tokenize(text)
    phrases = {}
    current_phrase = []
    for word in words:
        if (word in stopwords or word in \
            string.punctuation):
            if (len(current_phrase) > 1):
                phrases[" ".join(current_phrase)] = \
                "_".join(current_phrase)
                current_phrase = []
        else:
            current_phrase.append(word)
    if (len(current_phrase) > 1):
        phrases[" ".join(current_phrase)] = \
        "_".join(current_phrase)
    return phrases
```

5. The `replace_phrases` function takes a corpus of text and replace phrases with their underscored versions:

```python
def replace_phrases(phrases_dict, text):
    for phrase in phrases_dict.keys():
        text = text.replace(phrase, phrases_dict[phrase])
    return text
```

6. The `write_text_to_file` function takes a string and a filename as input and will write the text to the specified file:

```python
def write_text_to_file(text, filename):
    text_file = open(filename, "w", encoding="utf-8")
    text_file.write(text)
    text_file.close()
```

7. The `create_and_save_frequency_dist` function takes a word list and a filename as input, creates a frequency distribution, and pickles it to the provided file:

```
def create_and_save_frequency_dist(word_list, filename):
    fdist = FreqDist(word_list)
    pickle.dump(fdist, open(filename, 'wb'))
    return fdist
```

8. Now, we can use the preceding functions to discover and tag the phrases, and then train the model. First, read in the Yelp! reviews, find the phrases, and substitute the spaces in them with underscores in the original text. We can then save the transformed text to a file:

```
text = get_yelp_reviews(yelp_reviews_file)
phrases = get_phrases(text)
text = replace_phrases(phrases, text)
write_text_to_file(text, "Chapter03/all_text.txt")
```

9. Now, we will create a `FreqDist` object to look at the most common words and phrases. First, divide the text into sentences, then divide each sentence into words, and then create a flat word list instead of a list of lists (we will use the list of lists later to train the model):

```
sentences = divide_into_sentences_nltk(text)
all_sentence_words=[tokenize_nltk(sentence.lower()) for \
                    sentence in sentences]
flat_word_list = [word.lower() for sentence in \
                    all_sentence_words for word in
                    sentence]
fdist = \
create_and_save_frequency_dist(flat_word_list,
                    "Chapter03/fdist.bin")
```

10. We can print the most frequent words from the `FreqDist` object:

```
print(fdist.most_common()[:1000])
```

The result will be as follows:

```
[('.', 70799), ('the', 64657), (',', 49045), ('and',
40782), ('i', 38192), ('a', 35892), ('to', 26827),
('was', 23567), ('it', 21520), ('of', 19241), ('is',
16366), ('for', 15530), ('!', 14724), ('in', 14670),
('that', 12265), ('you', 11186), ('with', 10869), ('my',
10508), ('they', 10311), ('but', 9919), ('this', 9578),
('we', 9387), ("n't", 9016), ('on', 8951), ("'s", 8732),
('have', 8378), ('not', 7887), ('were', 6743), ('are',
6591), ('had', 6586), ('so', 6528), (')', 6251), ('at',
6243), ('as', 5898), ('(', 5563), ('there', 5341),
('me', 4819), ('be', 4567), ('if', 4465), ('here', 4459),
('just', 4401), ('all', 4357), ('out', 4241), ('like',
4216), ('very', 4138), ('do', 4064), ('or', 3759), …]
```

11. We will now train the `word2vec` model:

```
model = \
create_and_save_word2vec_model(all_sentence_words,
                        "Chapter03/phrases.model")
```

12. We can now test the model by looking at words that are the most similar to *highly recommend* and *happy hour*:

```
words = model.wv.most_similar("highly_recommend",
topn=10)
print(words)
words = model.wv.most_similar("happy_hour", topn=10)
print(words)
```

The result will be as follows:

```
[('recommend', 0.7311313152313232), ('would_definitely_
recommend', 0.7066166400909424), ('absolutely_
recommend', 0.6534838676452637), ('definitely_
recommend', 0.6242724657058716), ('absolutely_love',
0.5880271196365356), ('reccomend', 0.5669443011283875),
('highly_recommend_going', 0.5308369994163513),
('strongly_recommend', 0.5057551860809326), ('recommend_
kingsway_chiropractic', 0.5053386688232422),
('recommending', 0.5042617321014404)]

[('lunch', 0.5662612915039062), ('sushi',
0.5589481592178345), ('dinner', 0.5486307740211487),
('brunch', 0.5425440669059753), ('breakfast',
```

```
0.5249745845794678), ('restaurant_week',
0.4805092215538025), ('osmosis', 0.44396835565567017),
('happy_hour.wow', 0.4393075406551361), ('actual_
massage', 0.43787407875061035), ('friday_night',
0.4282568395137787)]
```

13. We can also test out less frequent phrases, such as *fried rice* and *dim sum*:

```
words = model.wv.most_similar("fried_rice", topn=10)
print(words)
words = model.wv.most_similar("dim_sum", topn=10)
print(words)
```

The result will be as follows:

```
[('pulled_pork', 0.5275152325630188), ('pork_belly',
0.5048087239265442), ('beef', 0.5020794868469238),
('hollandaise', 0.48470234870910645), ('chicken',
0.47735923528671265), ('rice', 0.4758814871311188),
('pork', 0.457661509513855), ('crab_rangoon',
0.4489888846874237), ('lasagna', 0.43910956382751465),
('lettuce_wraps', 0.4385792315006256)]
```

```
[('late_night', 0.4120914041996002), ('lunch',
0.4054332971572876), ('meal.we', 0.3739640414714813),
('tacos', 0.3505086302757263), ('breakfast',
0.34057727456092834), ('high_end_restaurant',
0.33562248945236206), ('cocktails', 0.3332172632217407),
('lunch_specials', 0.33315491676330566), ('longer_
period', 0.33072057366371155), ('bubble_tea',
0.32894694805145264)]
```

How it works...

Many of the processing steps in this recipe take a long time, and for that reason, we save the intermediate results to files.

In *step 1*, we import the necessary packages and functions. In *step 2*, we assign the variable definitions for the stopwords file and the Yelp! reviews file and then read in the stopwords.

In *step 3*, we define the `get_yelp_reviews` function, which reads in the reviews. The reviews file is 3.9 GB in size and might not fit into memory (or it will fit and slow down your computer immensely). In order to solve this problem, we can use the `pandas` `read_json` method, which lets us read a specified number of lines at once. In the code, I just used the first 10,000 lines, though there are many more. This method creates a `pandas` `Dataframe` object. We iterate through the rows of the object one by one and use the `langdetect` package to determine if the review text is in English. Then, we only include English reviews in the text.

In *step 4*, we define the `get_phrases` function. This function takes in the review corpus as input and detects that they are semantically one unit, such as *fried rice*. The function finds them by considering punctuation and stopwords as border tokens. Anything between them is considered a phrase. Once we've found all the phrases, we substitute spaces with underscores so that the `word2vec` module considers them as one token. The function returns a dictionary where the key is the input phrase with space(s) and the value is the phrase with an underscore.

In *step 5*, we define the `replace_phrases` function, which takes in the review corpus and replaces all the phrases from the `phrases_dict` object. Now, the corpus contains all the phrases with underscores in them.

In *step 6*, we define the `write_text_to_file` function, which will save the provided text to the file with the provided filename.

In *step 7*, we create the `create_and_save_frequency_dist` function, which creates a `FreqDist` object from the provided corpus and saves it to a file. The reason we create this function is to show that high frequency phrases, such as **highly recommend** and *happy hour*, have good results with `word2vec`, while with lower frequency phrases, such as *fried rice* and *dim sum*, the quality of similar words starts to decline. The solution would be to process larger quantities of data, which, of course, would slow down the tagging and training process.

In *step 8*, we create the text review corpus by using the `get_yelp_reviews` function. We then create the phrase dictionary by using the `get_phrases` function. Finally, we write the resulting corpus to a file.

In *step 9*, we create a `FreqDist` object, which will show us the most common words and phrases in the corpus. First, we divide the text into sentences. Then, we use a list comprehension to get all the words in the sentences. After that, we flatten the resulting double list and also lowercase all the words. Finally, we use the `create_and_save_frequency_dist` function to create the `FreqDist` object.

In *step 10*, we print the most common words and phrases from the frequency distribution. The result shows the most common words in the corpus. Your numbers and the order of the words might be different, as the Yelp dataset is regularly updated. In *steps 11* and *12*, you can use other phrases that are more or less frequent in your results.

In *step 11*, we train the `word2vec` model. In *step 12*, we print out the words that are the most similar to the phrases *highly recommend* and *happy hour*. These phrases are frequent and the similar words are indeed similar, where *recommend* and *would definitely recommend* are the most similar phrases to *highly recommend*.

In *step 13*, we print out the most similar words to the phrases *fried rice* and *dim sum*. Since these a lower frequency phrases, we can see that the words that are returned by the model as the most similar are very similar to the input.

One of the intermediate steps is creating a frequency distribution.

See also

Kavita Ganesan made a Python package for extracting phrases from large corpora using PySpark, and her code is available at `https://github.com/kavgan/phrase-at-scale/`. You can read about her approach at her blog at `https://kavita-ganesan.com/how-to-incorporate-phrases-into-word2vec-a-text-mining-approach/`.

Using BERT instead of word embeddings

A recent development in the embeddings world is **BERT**, also known as **Bidirectional Encoder Representations from Transformers**, which, like word embeddings, gives a vector representation, but it takes context into account and can represent a whole sentence. We can use the Hugging Face `sentence_transformers` package to represent sentences as vectors.

Getting ready

For this recipe, we need to install PyTorch with Torchvision, and then the transformers and sentence transformers from Hugging Face. Follow these installation steps in an Anaconda prompt. For Windows, use the following code:

```
conda install pytorch torchvision cudatoolkit=10.2 -c pytorch
pip install transformers
pip install -U sentence-transformers
```

For macOS, use the following code:

```
conda install pytorch torchvision torchaudio -c pytorch
pip install transformers
pip install -U sentence-transformers
```

How to do it...

The Hugging Face code makes using BERT very easy. The first time the code runs, it will download the necessary model, which might take some time. Once you've downloaded it, it's just a matter of encoding the sentences using the model. We will use the `sherlock_holmes_1.txt` file we've used previously for this. Let's get started:

1. Import the `SentenceTransformer` class and helper methods:

    ```
    from sentence_transformers import SentenceTransformer
    from Chapter01.dividing_into_sentences import read_text_file, \
    divide_into_sentences_nltk
    ```

2. Read the text file and divide the text into sentences:

    ```
    text = read_text_file("sherlock_holmes.txt")
    sentences = divide_into_sentences_nltk(text)
    ```

3. Load the sentence transformer model:

    ```
    model = SentenceTransformer('bert-base-nli-mean-tokens')
    ```

4. Get the sentence embeddings:

    ```
    sentence_embeddings = model.encode(sentences)
    ```

    The result will be as follows:

    ```
    [[-0.41089028  1.1092614   0.653306   ... -0.9232089
    0.4728682
         0.36298898]
     [-0.16485551  0.6998439   0.7076392  ... -0.40428287
    -0.30385852
       -0.3291511 ]
     [-0.37814915  0.34771013 -0.09765357 ...  0.13831234
    0.3604408
    ```

```
    0.12382    ]

 ...

  [-0.25148678   0.5758055    1.4596572   ...    0.56890184
-0.6003894

   -0.02739916]
  [-0.64917654   0.3609671    1.1350367   ...  -0.04054655
0.07568665

   0.1809447 ]
  [-0.4241825    0.48146117   0.93001956  ...   0.73677135
-0.09357803

   -0.0036802 ]]
```

5. We can also encode a part of a sentence, such as a noun chunk:

```
sentence_embeddings = model.encode(["the beautiful
lake"])
```
```
print(sentence_embeddings)
```

The result will be as follows:

```
[[-7.61981383e-02 -5.74670374e-01   1.08264232e+00
7.36554384e-01

     5.51345229e-01 -9.39117730e-01 -2.80430615e-01
-5.41626096e-01

     7.50949085e-01 -4.40971524e-01   5.31526923e-01
-5.41883349e-01

     1.92792594e-01   3.44117582e-01   1.50266397e+00
-6.26989722e-01

    -2.42828876e-01 -3.66734862e-01   5.57459474e-01
-2.21802562e-01 …]]
```

How it works...

The sentence transformer's BERT model is a pre-trained model, just like a word2vec model, that encodes a sentence into a vector. The difference between a word2vec model and a sentence transformer model is that we encode sentences in the latter, and not words.

In *step 1*, we import the SentenceTransformer object and the helper functions. In *step 2*, we read in the text of the sherlock_holmes_1.txt file and divide it into sentences. In *step 3*, we load the pretrained model and in *step 4*, we load the vectors for each of the sentences in the text. In *step 5*, we encode the phrase *the beautiful lake*. Since the encode function expects a list, we create a one-element list.

Once we've encoded the sentences using the model, we can use them in a downstream task, such as classification or sentiment analysis.

Getting started with semantic search

In this recipe, we will get a glimpse of how to get started on expanding search with the help of a word2vec model. When we search for a term, we expect the search engine to show us a result with a synonym when we didn't use the exact term contained in the document. Search engines are far more complicated than what we'll show in the recipe, but this should give you a taste of what it's like to build a customizable search engine.

Getting ready

We will be using an IMDb dataset from Kaggle, which can be downloaded from https://www.kaggle.com/PromptCloudHQ/imdb-data. Download the dataset and unzip the CSV file.

We will also use a small-scale Python search engine called Whoosh. Install it using pip:

```
pip install whoosh
```

We will also be using the pretrained word2vec model from the *Using word embeddings* recipe.

How to do it...

We will create a class for the Whoosh search engine that will create a document index based on the IMDb file. Then, we will load the pretrained word2vec model and use it to augment the queries we pass to the engine. Let's get started:

1. Import the helper methods and classes:

    ```
    from whoosh.fields import import Schema, TEXT, KEYWORD, ID,
    STORED, DATETIME
    from whoosh.index import create_in
    from whoosh.analysis import StemmingAnalyzer
    from whoosh.qparser import MultifieldParser
    import csv
    from Chapter03.word_embeddings import w2vec_model_path
    from Chapter03.word_embeddings import load_model
    ```

2. Create a directory called `whoosh_index` in the `Chapter03` folder. Then, set the paths for the search engine index and the IMDb dataset path:

```
imdb_dataset_path = "Chapter03/IMDB-Movie-Data.csv"
search_engine_index_path = "Chapter03/whoosh_index"
```

3. Create the `IMDBSearchEngine` class. The complete code for this class can be found in this book's GitHub repository. The most important part of it is the `query_engine` function:

```
class IMDBSearchEngine:

    ...


    def query_engine(self, keywords):
        with self.index.searcher() as searcher:
            query=\
            MultifieldParser(["title", "description"],
                                self.index.schema).\
                                parse(keywords)
            results = searcher.search(query)
            print(results)
            print(results[0])
            return results
```

4. The `get_similar_words` function takes a word and the pretrained model and returns the top three words that are similar to the given word:

```
def get_similar_words(model, search_term):
    similarity_list = model.most_similar(search_term,
topn=3)
    similar_words = [sim_tuple[0] for sim_tuple in \
                        similarity_list]
    return similar_words
```

5. Now, we can initialize the search engine. Use the first line to initialize the search engine when the index doesn't exist yet, and the second line when you've already created it once:

```
search_engine = \
IMDBSearchEngine(search_engine_index_path,
```

```
                    imdb_dataset_path,
                    load_existing=False)
#search_engine = \
IMDBSearchEngine(search_engine_index_path,
                    load_existing=True)
```

6. Load the word2vec model:

```
model = load_model(w2vec_model_path)
```

7. Let's say a user wants to find the movie *Colossal*, but forgot its real name, so they search for *gigantic*. We will use *gigantic* as the search term:

```
search_term = "gigantic"
```

8. We will get three words similar to the input word:

```
other_words = get_similar_words(model, search_term)
```

9. We will then query the engine to return all the movies containing those words:

```
results = \
search_engine.query_engine(" OR ".join([search_term] +
                            other_words))
print(results[0])
```

10. The result will be the movie with an ID of 15, which is the movie *Colossal*:

```
<Hit {'movie_id': '15'}>
```

How it works...

In *step 1*, we import the necessary packages and functions. In *step 2*, we initialize the dataset and search engine paths. Make sure to create a directory called whoosh_index in the Chapter03 folder.

In *step 3*, we create the IMDBSearchEngine class. The constructor takes the following arguments: the path to the search engine index, the path to the CSV dataset, which is an empty string by default, and the load_existing boolean argument, which is False by default. If load_existing is False, imdb_path needs to point to the dataset. In this case, a new index will be created at the path provided by the index_path variable. If load_existing is True, the imdb_path variable is ignored, and the existing index is loaded from index_path.

All the indices are created using a schema, and this search engine's schema is created in the `create_schema` function. The schema specifies which fields the information about the document will contain. In this case, it is the movie's title, its description, genre, director, actors, and year of release. The document index is then created using the `populate_index` function. Once the index has been populated, we do not need to reindex it, and can open the index from disk.

The `query_engine` function searches the index with the keywords that are sent to it. When creating a query parser, we use the `MultifieldParser` class so that we can search through multiple fields; in this case, title and description.

In *step 4*, we create the `get_similar_words` function, which returns the top three words that are similar to the word being passed in using a `word2vec` model. This should be familiar from the *Using word embeddings* recipe. The function gets the list of word similarity score tuples and returns a list of words.

In *step 5*, we create the `search_engine` object. There are two lines, the first one creates a new search engine from scratch, while the second one loads an existing index. You should run the first line the first time and the second line every other time after that.

In *step 6*, we load the `word2vec` model.

In *step 7*, we set the search term to *gigantic*. In *step 8*, we get the top three similar words for the initial search term using the `get_similar_words` function. In *step 9*, we use the `search_engine` object to perform the search using the original search term and the similar words as the query. The result is movie number 15, *Colossal*, which is the correct answer.

See also

Please refer to the official Whoosh documentation to explore how it's used. It can be found at `https://whoosh.readthedocs.io/en/latest/`.

4
Classifying Texts

In this chapter, we will be classifying texts using different methods. After reading this chapter, you will be able to preprocess and classify texts using keywords, unsupervised clustering, and two supervised algorithms: **support vector machines (SVMs)** and **long short-term memory neural networks (LSTMs)**.

Here is the list of recipes in this chapter:

- Getting the dataset and evaluation baseline ready
- Performing rule-based text classification using keywords
- Clustering sentences using K-means: unsupervised text classification
- Using SVMs for supervised text classification
- Using LSTMs for supervised text classification

Technical requirements

The code for this chapter is located in a folder named Chapter04 in the GitHub repository for the book (https://github.com/PacktPublishing/Python-Natural-Language-Processing-Cookbook). There will be a few packages that we will need to install: numpy, sklearn, pandas, tensorflow, keras, and tqdm. Install them using these commands:

```
pip install numpy
```
```
pip install sklearn
```
```
pip install pandas
```
```
pip install tensorflow
```
```
pip install keras
```
```
pip install tqdm
```

Please also follow the individual recipe instructions to get the datasets.

Getting the dataset and evaluation baseline ready

Classifying texts is a classic NLP problem. This NLP task involves assigning a value to a text, for example, a topic or a sentiment, and any such task requires evaluation. In this recipe, we will load a dataset, prepare it for processing, and create an evaluation baseline. The recipe builds on some of the recipes from *Chapter 3, Representing Text: Capturing Semantics*, where we used different tools to represent text in a computer-readable form.

Getting ready

For most recipes in this chapter, we will use the BBC News dataset, which contains text from five topics: business, entertainment, politics, sport, and tech. The dataset is located in the bbc-text.csv file in this chapter's GitHub directory.

In this recipe, we will need two additional packages, numpy and sklearn. Install them using pip:

```
pip install numpy
```
```
pip install sklearn
```

How to do it...

In this recipe, we will be classifying just two of the five topics, sport and business. We will load the dataset from the provided CSV file and format it into a `numpy` array. We will then use the `TfidfVectorizer` class, which you might remember from the previous chapter, to represent the texts as vectors.

Here are the steps:

1. Do the necessary imports:

```
import csv
import nltk
import string
import numpy as np
from nltk.probability import FreqDist
from sklearn.feature_extraction.text import
TfidfVectorizer
from sklearn.metrics import classification_report
from sklearn.model_selection import train_test_split
from sklearn.dummy import DummyClassifier
from sklearn import preprocessing
from nltk.stem.snowball import SnowballStemmer
from Chapter01.tokenization import tokenize_nltk
```

2. Initialize the global variables:

```
stemmer = SnowballStemmer('english')
bbc_dataset = "Chapter04/bbc-text.csv"
stopwords_file_path = "Chapter01/stopwords.csv"
stopwords = []
```

3. We will use the following function to read in the CSV files:

```
def read_in_csv(csv_file):
    with open(csv_file, 'r', encoding='utf-8') as fp:
        reader = csv.reader(fp, delimiter=',',
                            quotechar='"')
        data_read = [row for row in reader]
    return data_read
```

4. We will use another function to tokenize and stem words, including stopwords:

```
def tokenize_and_stem(sentence):
    tokens = nltk.word_tokenize(sentence)
    filtered_tokens = [t for t in tokens if t not in
                        string.punctuation]
    stems = [stemmer.stem(t) for t in filtered_tokens]
    return stems
```

5. Here is the function to get the stopwords:

```
def get_stopwords(path=stopwords_file_path):
    stopwords = read_in_csv(path)
    stopwords = [word[0] for word in stopwords]
    stemmed_stopwords = [stemmer.stem(word) for word in
                         stopwords]
    stopwords = stopwords + stemmed_stopwords
    return stopwords
```

6. We can immediately use the get_stopwords function to fill the stopwords list:

```
stopwords = get_stopwords(stopwords_file_path)
```

7. The get_data function will represent the input data as a dictionary:

```
def get_data(filename):
    data = read_in_csv(filename)
    data_dict = {}
    for row in data[1:]:
        category = row[0]
        text = row[1]
        if (category not in data_dict.keys()):
            data_dict[category] = []
        data_dict[category].append(text)
    return data_dict
```

8. We can print out the number of texts for each topic with the following code:

```
for topic in data_dict.keys():
    print(topic, "\t", len(data_dict[topic]))
```

The result will be as follows:

```
tech        401
business          510
sport       511
entertainment     386
politics          417
```

9. The `get_stats` function will return a `FreqDist` object that will provide the top words used in the text:

```
def get_stats(text, num_words=200):
    word_list = tokenize_nltk(text)
    word_list = [word for word in word_list if word
                 not in stopwords and re.search(
                                "[A-Za-z]", word)]
    freq_dist = FreqDist(word_list)
    print(freq_dist.most_common(num_words))
    return freq_dist
```

10. We can now use the preceding functions to get the business and sport text and see the differences in their vocabulary:

```
data_dict = get_data(bbc_dataset)
business_data = data_dict["business"]
sports_data = data_dict["sport"]
business_string = " ".join(business_data)
sports_string = " ".join(sports_data)
get_stats(business_string)
get_stats(sports_string)
```

The output will look as follows – business first and then sport:

```
[('year', 637), ('market', 425), ('new', 416),
('company', 415), ('growth', 384), ('last', 365),
('firm', 362), ('economy', 359), ('government', 340),
('bank', 335), ('sales', 316), ('economic', 310),
('oil', 294), ('shares', 265), ('world', 252), ('years',
247), ('prices', 246), ('chief', 236), ('china', 223),
('business', 218), ('companies', 212), ('analysts', 209),
('uk', 207), ('deal', 206), ('rise', 203), ('expected',
200), ('group', 199), ('financial', 197), ('yukos',
```

```
196), ('firms', 193), ('dollar', 180), ('december',
173), ('country', 173), ('months', 170), ('people',
170), ('stock', 168), ('first', 165), ('president',
165), ('three', 164), ('time', 159), ('european', 159),
('rate', 159), ('state', 158), ('trade', 158), ('told',
155), ('investment', 153), ('demand', 151), ('interest',
151),…]
```

```
[('game', 476), ('england', 459), ('first', 437),
('win', 415), ('world', 379), ('last', 376), ('time',
327), ('back', 318), ('players', 307), ('play', 292),
('cup', 290), ('new', 285), ('m', 280), ('o', 276),
('side', 270), ('ireland', 270), ('year', 267), ('team',
265), ('wales', 265), ('good', 258), ('club', 254),
('six', 246), ('match', 245), ('won', 241), ('three',
230), ('set', 228), ('final', 228), ('coach', 228),
('france', 227), ('season', 223), ('get', 212), ('rugby',
210), ('injury', 208), ('think', 204), ('take', 201),
('chelsea', 201), ('added', 200), ('great', 191),
('open', 181), ('victory', 180), ('best', 178), ('years',
177), ('next', 174), ('told', 174), ('league', 172),
('games', 171), …]
```

11. We will use the `create_vectorizer` function to create a TFIDF vectorizer for the text:

```
def create_vectorizer(text_list):

    tfidf_vectorizer = \
    TfidfVectorizer(max_df=0.90, max_features=200000,
                    min_df=0.05, stop_words='english',
                    use_idf=True,
                    tokenizer=tokenize_and_stem,
                    ngram_range=(1,3))
    tfidf_vectorizer.fit_transform(text_list)
    return tfidf_vectorizer
```

12. We will use the `split_test_train` function to split the dataset into a training and a test set:

```
def split_test_train(data, train_percent):
    train_test_border = \
    math.ceil(train_percent*len(data))
```

```
    train_data = data[0:train_test_border]
    test_data = data[train_test_border:]
    return (train_data, test_data)
```

13. Now we will split both the business and sports news to get training and test data for both of them and create a vectorizer just using the training data:

```
(business_train_data, business_test_data) = \
  split_test_train(business_data, 0.8)
(sports_train_data, sports_test_data) = \
  split_test_train(sports_data, 0.8)
train_data = business_train_data + sports_train_data
tfidf_vec = create_vectorizer(train_data)
```

14. With the help of the preceding function, we get the label encoder:

```
le = get_labels(["business", "sport"])
```

15. We will use the create_dataset function to transform the text data into a numpy array:

```
def create_dataset(vectorizer, data_dict, le):
    business_news = data_dict["business"]
    sports_news = data_dict["sport"]
    (sports_vectors, sports_labels) = \
      create_data_matrix(sports_news, vectorizer,
                         "sport", le)
    (business_vectors, business_labels) = \
      create_data_matrix(business_news, vectorizer,
                         "business", le)
    all_data_matrix = np.vstack((business_vectors,
                                 sports_vectors))
    labels = np.concatenate([business_labels,
                             sports_labels])
    return (all_data_matrix, labels)
```

16. The `create_dataset` function uses the `create_data_matrix` helper function, which encodes the text using the vectorizer and the labels using the `LabelEncoder` object:

```
def create_data_matrix(input_data, vectorizer, label,
le):
    vectors = \
    vectorizer.transform(input_data).todense()
    labels = [label]*len(input_data)
    enc_labels = le.transform(labels)
    return (vectors, enc_labels)
```

17. We now create two data dictionaries, a training and a test dictionary, and then create the training and test datasets:

```
train_data_dict = {'business':business_train_data,
                   'sport':sports_train_data}
test_data_dict = {'business':business_test_data,
                  'sport':sports_test_data}
(X_train, y_train) = \
create_dataset(tfidf_vec, train_data_dict, le)
(X_test, y_test) = \
create_dataset(tfidf_vec, test_data_dict, le)
```

18. We will now create a dummy classifier that assigns classes randomly and uniformly. We will use the `predict_trivial` function to establish a baseline for the classifiers we build in the next recipes:

```
def predict_trivial(X_train, y_train, X_test, y_test,
le):
    dummy_clf = DummyClassifier(strategy='uniform',
                               random_state=0)
    dummy_clf.fit(X_train, y_train)
    y_pred = dummy_clf.predict(X_test)
    print(dummy_clf.score(X_test, y_test))
    print(classification_report(y_test, y_pred,
        labels=le.transform(le.classes_),
        target_names=le.classes_))
```

19. We now use the `predict_trivial` function on our dataset:

```
predict_trivial(X_train, y_train, X_test, y_test, le)
```

The result will be as follows:

	precision	recall	f1-score	support
business	0.45	0.44	0.44	102
sport	0.45	0.45	0.45	102
accuracy			0.45	204
macro avg	0.45	0.45	0.45	204
weighted avg	0.45	0.45	0.45	204

How it works...

The program does the following things:

1. Reads in the BBC topic dataset

2. Represents its text as vectors using the TFIDF vectorizer

3. Represents the topic labels as numbers

4. Analyzes the number of texts available for each topic and the most frequent words for the two most numerous topics

5. Trains a dummy classifier on the data

In *step 1*, we import the necessary packages and functions. In *step 2*, we initialize the global variables. In *step 3*, we define the `read_in_csv` function, which reads in the file and returns the data as a list. In *step 4*, we define the `tokenize_and_stem` function, which reads in a sentence, splits it into words, removes tokens that are punctuation, and finally stems the resulting tokens.

In *step 5*, we define the `get_stopwords` function, which reads in the stopwords file and returns the stopwords in a list, and in *step 6* we use it to get the stopwords list.

In *step 7*, we define the `get_data` function, which turns the CSV input into a dictionary, where the keys are the five topics and the values are lists of texts for that topic.

In *step 8*, we print out the number of texts for each topic. Since business and sports have the most examples, we use these two topics for classification.

In *step 9*, we create the `get_stats` function. In the function, we tokenize the text, then remove all stopwords and words that include characters other than letters of the English alphabet, and finally we create a `FreqDist` object, which provides information about the most frequent words in a text. In *step 10*, we get the data and compare business and sports news using the `get_stats` function. We see that the distributions are quite different for business and sport, although there are some frequent words that they share, such as `world`.

In *step 11*, we define the `create_vectorizer` function, which will encode our texts as vectors for use with the classifier. In it, we use the `TfidfVectorizer` class as in *Chapter 3, Representing Text: Capturing Semantics*. In *step 12*, we create the `split_test_train` function, which will split the dataset into training and test sets. The function takes in the data and a percent of the data to be used as training. It calculates the border where the list needs to be split and uses that to create two lists, one training and the other test.

In *step 13*, we split both the business and sport news lists with 80% of the data reserved for training and 20% for testing. We then create the vectorizer including both business and sports news. The creation of the classifier is part of the training process, and thus only training data is used.

In *step 14*, we create the label encoder that will transform text labels into numbers using the `LabelEncoder` class. In *step 15*, we define the `create_dataset` function, which takes in the vectorizer, the input data dictionary, and the label encoder and creates `numpy` arrays of vector-encoded text and labels for both business and sports news.

In *step 16*, we define the `create_data_matrix` function, which is a helper function to `create_dataset`. It takes in a list of texts, the vectorizer, the label being used, and the label encoder. It then creates the vector representation of the text using the vectorizer. It also creates a list of labels and then encodes them using the label encoder.

In *step 17*, we create a training and a test data dictionary and create the training and test datasets using the `create_dataset` function. In *step 18*, we define the `predict_trivial` function, which the `DummyClassifier` class that predicts the labels for the news items. We use the uniform strategy, which generates predictions uniformly at random. We then use the `classification_report` method from the `sklearn` class to do a standard evaluation that computes accuracy, recall, precision, and F1.

In *step 19*, we use the `predict_trivial` function on our dataset. The scores show us that the dummy classifier gets roughly 45% of the answers correct, a little below random chance.

Performing rule-based text classification using keywords

In this recipe, we will use the keywords to classify the business and sport data. We will create a classifier with keywords that we will choose by ourselves from the frequency distributions from the previous recipe.

Getting ready

We will continue using classes from the `sklearn`, `numpy`, and `nltk` packages that we used in the previous recipe.

How to do it...

In this recipe, we will use hand-picked business and sport vocabulary to create a keyword classifier that we will evaluate using the same method as the dummy classifier in the previous recipe. The steps for this recipe are as follows:

1. Do the necessary imports:

```
import numpy as np
import string
from sklearn import preprocessing
from sklearn.metrics import classification_report
from sklearn.model_selection import train_test_split
from sklearn.feature_extraction.text import
CountVectorizer
from itertools import repeat
from nltk.probability import FreqDist
from Chapter01.tokenization import tokenize_nltk
from Chapter04.preprocess_bbc_dataset import get_data
from Chapter04.preprocess_bbc_dataset import get_
stopwords
```

2. After examining the 200 most frequent words from the business and sport vocabularies, we manually pick vocabularies for sport and business:

```
business_vocabulary = ["market", "company", "growth",
"firm", "economy", "government", "bank", "sales", "oil",
"prices", "business", "uk", "financial", "dollar",
"stock","trade", "investment", "quarter", "profit",
```

```
"jobs", "foreign", "tax","euro", "budget", "cost",
"money", "investor", "industry", "million", "debt"]
sports_vocabulary = ["game", "england", "win", "player",
"cup", "team", "club", "match","set", "final",
"coach", "season", "injury", "victory", "league",
"play","champion", "olympic", "title", "ball", "sport",
"race", "football", "rugby","tennis", "basketball",
"hockey"]
```

3. We will now create two different vectorizers, one for sport and one for business:

```
business_vectorizer = \
CountVectorizer(vocabulary=business_vocabulary)
sports_vectorizer = \
CountVectorizer(vocabulary=sports_vocabulary)
```

4. Initialize the other global variables:

```
bbc_dataset = "Chapter04/bbc-text.csv"
stopwords_file_path = "Chapter01/stopwords.csv"
stopwords = get_stopwords(stopwords_file_path)
```

5. Define a function to create the label encoder and create it:

```
def get_labels(labels):
    le = preprocessing.LabelEncoder()
    le.fit(labels)
    return le
le = get_labels(["business", "sport"])
```

6. The create_dataset function will create a numpy array from the data:

```
def create_dataset(data_dict, le):
    data_matrix = []
    classifications = []
    gold_labels = []
    for text in data_dict["business"]:
        gold_labels.append(le.transform(["business"]))
        text_vector = transform(text)
        data_matrix.append(text_vector)
    for text in data_dict["sport"]:
```

```
            gold_labels.append(le.transform(["sport"]))
            text_vector = transform(text)
            data_matrix.append(text_vector)
    X = np.array(data_matrix)
    y = np.array(gold_labels)
    return (X, y)
```

7. The `transform` function will take in text and transform it into a vector:

```
def transform(text):
    business_X = business_vectorizer.transform([text])
    sports_X = sports_vectorizer.transform([text])
    business_sum = \
    sum(business_X.todense().tolist()[0])
    sports_sum = sum(sports_X.todense().tolist()[0])
    return np.array([business_sum, sports_sum])
```

8. We will now define the `classify` function, which will assign a `sports` or `business` label to the input text:

```
def classify(vector, le):
    label = ""
    if (vector[0] > vector[1]):
        label = "business"
    else:
        label = "sport"
    return le.transform([label])
```

9. The `evaluate` function will evaluate the performance of our classifier:

```
def evaluate(X, y):
    y_pred = np.array(list(map(classify, X,
                              repeat(le))))
    print(classification_report(y, y_pred,
        labels=le.transform(le.classes_),
        target_names=le.classes_))
```

10. We can now use the preceding functions to evaluate our classifier on all the data provided:

```
data_dict = get_data(bbc_dataset)
(X, y) = create_dataset(data_dict, le)
evaluate(X, y)
```

The result will be as follows:

	precision	recall	f1-score	support
business	1.00	0.98	0.99	510
sport	0.98	1.00	0.99	511
accuracy			0.99	1021
macro avg	0.99	0.99	0.99	1021
weighted avg	0.99	0.99	0.99	1021

How it works...

In *step 1*, we import the necessary functions and packages. In *step 2*, we define the vocabularies for business and sports to later use them in business and sports vectorizers. We selected the most representative words for each category by looking at the top 200 words data from the previous recipe. I did not use words that appear in both categories, such as `world`.

In *step 3*, we create the two vectorizers, one for business and one for sports using the vocabularies defined in *step 2*. In *step 4*, we initialize other global variables. In *step 5*, we define the `get_labels` function, which creates a label encoder given an input list of labels, and then use the function to define the label encoder.

In *step 6*, we define the `create_dataset` function, which will take in a data dictionary and a label encoder and create the data matrix and a label array. It encodes each news item as a vector and transforms labels using the label encoder. Both vectorizers are used on each news piece and their data is combined into one vector.

In *step 7*, we define the `transform` function. This function transforms an input text into a vector of two elements. It first applies the business and sports vectorizers to the text. These results provide counts of business and sports vocabulary in the text. We then sum both of those and each sum becomes one of the elements in the final vector. The first element is the count of business vocabulary, and the second element is the count of sports vocabulary.

In *step 8*, we define the function classify that takes in a vector and assigns it a label, either sports or business. The function takes as input a vector created by the transform function and compares the first element to the second. If the first element is greater than the second, or there are more business words in the input text than there are sports words, it assigns it the business label. If there are more sports words, it assigns it a sports label. If the two counts are equal, the sports label is assigned. The function then returns the output label encoded with the label encoder.

In *step 9*, we define the evaluate function. The function takes in the input matrix and the label array. It then creates the y_pred array, or the array of predictions for each of the vectors in the input matrix. It does that by applying the classify function to the input. It then prints out the classification report by comparing the right answers in y to the predicted answers in y_pred.

In *step 10*, we create the data dictionary from the input, then create the dataset and evaluate the result. We then run the classification_report function on the data and get 99% accuracy.

There's more...

Instead of hand-picking the vocabulary for the vectorizers, we can automate the process. We will use automated keyword classification for all five topics in this section. Here is how to do it:

1. Get the data:

```
data_dict = get_data(bbc_dataset)
```

2. We will define the divide_data function to randomly split the data into training and test sets:

```
def divide_data(data_dict):
    train_dict = {}
    test_dict = {}
    for topic in data_dict.keys():
        text_list = data_dict[topic]
        x_train, x_test = \
        train_test_split(text_list, test_size=0.2)
        train_dict[topic] = x_train
        test_dict[topic] = x_test
    return (train_dict, test_dict)
```

3. Use the following function to divide the data:

```
(train_dict, test_dict) = divide_data(data_dict)
```

4. Get the labels:

```
le = get_labels(list(data_dict.keys()))
```

5. The `create_vectorizers` function will create a dictionary of vectorizers by topic:

```
def create_vectorizers(data_dict):
    topic_list = list(data_dict.keys())
    vectorizer_dict = {}
    for topic in topic_list:
        text_array = data_dict[topic]
        text = " ".join(text_array)
        word_list = tokenize_nltk(text)
        word_list = [word for word in word_list if
                        word not in stopwords]
        freq_dist = FreqDist(word_list)
        top_200 = freq_dist.most_common(200)
        vocab = [wtuple[0] for wtuple in top_200 if
                    wtuple[0] not in stopwords and
                    wtuple[0] not in string.punctuation]
        vectorizer_dict[topic] = \
        CountVectorizer(vocabulary=vocab)
    return vectorizer_dict
```

6. The `transform_auto` function will use the vectorizers to create a vector with word counts for each of the topics:

```
def transform_auto(text, vect_dict, le):
    number_topics = len(list(vect_dict.keys()))
    sum_list = [0]*number_topics
    for topic in vect_dict.keys():
        vectorizer = vect_dict[topic]
        this_topic_matrix = \
        vectorizer.transform([text])
        this_topic_sum = \
```

```
        sum(this_topic_matrix.todense().tolist()[0])
        index = le.transform([topic])[0]
        sum_list[index] = this_topic_sum
    return np.array(sum_list)
```

7. The `create_dataset_auto` function will use the vectorizer and data dictionaries to create the dataset in two numpy arrays:

```
def create_dataset_auto(data_dict, le, vectorizer_dict):
    data_matrix = []
    classifications = []
    gold_labels = []
    for topic in data_dict.keys():
        for text in data_dict[topic]:
            gold_labels.append(le.transform([topic]))
            text_vector = \
            transform_auto(text, vectorizer_dict, le)
            data_matrix.append(text_vector)
    X = np.array(data_matrix)
    y = np.array(gold_labels)
    return (X, y)
```

8. The `classify_auto` function will classify the input vector by picking the label that corresponds to the highest count of words:

```
def classify_auto(vector, le):
    result = np.where(vector == np.amax(vector))
    label = result[0][0]
    return [label]
```

9. The `evaluate_auto` function will evaluate the result:

```
def evaluate_auto(X, y, le):
    y_pred = np.array(list(map(classify_auto, X,
                          repeat(le))))
    print(classification_report(y, y_pred,
        labels=le.transform(le.classes_),
        target_names=le.classes_))
```

10. We will now run the defined functions and evaluate the result:

```
vectorizers = create_vectorizers(train_dict)
(X, y) = create_dataset_auto(test_dict, le,
                             vectorizers)
evaluate_auto(X, y, le)
```

The statistics will be as follows:

	precision	recall	f1-score	support
business	0.91	0.93	0.92	102
entertainment	0.96	0.90	0.93	78
politics	0.91	0.96	0.94	84
sport	0.98	1.00	0.99	103
tech	0.95	0.90	0.92	81
accuracy			0.94	448
macro avg	0.94	0.94	0.94	448
weighted avg	0.94	0.94	0.94	448

Even when we don't handpick the keywords, the resulting accuracy is 94%.

The main difference between the two recipes for keyword-based classification is that in this last piece of code, we use the most frequent words in each of the five topics to create the vectorizers that later encode the data, while in the first piece of code we had manually handpicked the vocabulary for the vectorizers. Also, here we classified all five topics as opposed to just business and sport in the first piece of code.

Clustering sentences using K-means – unsupervised text classification

In this recipe, we will use the same data as in the previous chapter and use the unsupervised K-means algorithm to sort data. After you have read this recipe, you will be able to create your own unsupervised clustering model that will sort data into several classes. You can then later apply it to any text data without having to first label it.

Getting ready

We will use the packages from the previous recipes, as well as the pandas package. Install it using pip:

```
pip install pandas
```

How to do it...

In this recipe, we will preprocess the data, vectorize it, and then cluster it using K-means. Since there are usually no right answers for unsupervised modeling, evaluating the models is more difficult, but we will be able to look at some statistics, as well as the most common words in all the clusters.

Your steps are as follows:

1. Import the necessary functions and packages:

```
import nltk
import re
import string
import pandas as pd
from sklearn.cluster import KMeans
from nltk.stem.snowball import SnowballStemmer
from sklearn.feature_extraction.text import
TfidfVectorizer
from nltk.probability import FreqDist
from Chapter01.tokenization import tokenize_nltk
from Chapter01.dividing_into_sentences import divide_
into_sentences_nltk
from Chapter04.preprocess_bbc_dataset import get_data
from Chapter04.keyword_classification import divide_data
from Chapter04.preprocess_bbc_dataset import get_
stopwords
```

2. Initialize the global variables:

```
bbc_dataset = "Chapter04/bbc-text.csv"
stopwords_file_path = "Chapter01/stopwords.csv"
stopwords = get_stopwords(stopwords_file_path)
stemmer = SnowballStemmer('english')
```

3. Get the data and divide it into training and testing data:

```
data_dict = get_data(bbc_dataset)
(train_dict, test_dict) = divide_data(data_dict)
```

4. Create text lists for training and test data:

```
all_training = []
all_test = []
for topic in train_dict.keys():
    all_training = all_training + train_dict[topic]
for topic in test_dict.keys():
    all_test = all_test + test_dict[topic]
```

5. We will use the `tokenize_and_stem` function when creating the vectorizer:

```
def tokenize_and_stem(sentence):
    tokens = nltk.word_tokenize(sentence)
    filtered_tokens = [t for t in tokens if t not in
                            stopwords and t not in
                            string.punctuation and
                            re.search('[a-zA-Z]', t)]
    stems = [stemmer.stem(t) for t in filtered_tokens]
    return stems
```

6. The `create_vectorizer` function will create and fit the vectorizer on the provided data:

```
def create_vectorizer(data):
    vec = \
    TfidfVectorizer(max_df=0.90, max_features=200000,
                        min_df=0.05, stop_words=stopwords,
                        use_idf=True,
                        tokenizer=tokenize_and_stem,
                        ngram_range=(1,3))
    vec.fit(data)
    return vec
```

7. We will now create the vectorizer and get the vector matrix for the training data:

```
vectorizer = create_vectorizer(all_training)
matrix = vectorizer.transform(all_training)
```

8. Now we can create the KMeans classifier for five clusters and then fit it on the matrix produced using the vectorizer from the preceding code:

```
km = KMeans(n_clusters=5, init='k-means++',
            random_state=0)
km.fit(matrix)
```

9. The make_predictions function will return a list of cluster numbers for unseen data:

```
def make_predictions(test_data, vectorizer, km):
    predicted_data = {}
    for topic in test_data.keys():
        this_topic_list = test_data[topic]
        if (topic not in predicted_data.keys()):
            predicted_data[topic] = {}
        for text in this_topic_list:
            prediction = \
            km.predict(vectorizer.transform([text]))[0]
            if (prediction not in \
                predicted_data[topic].keys()):
                predicted_data[topic][prediction] = []
            predicted_data[topic][prediction].
append(text)
        return predicted_data
```

10. We will use the print_report function to show the statistics about the model:

```
def print_report(predicted_data):
    for topic in predicted_data.keys():
        print(topic)
        for prediction in \
        predicted_data[topic].keys():
            print("Cluster number: ", prediction,
```

```
                              "number of items: ",
                        len(predicted_data[topic][prediction]))
```

11. Now we will use the `make_predictions` function on test data and print the report:

```
predicted_data = make_predictions(test_dict,
                                  vectorizer, km)
print_report(predicted_data)
```

The results will vary each time you run the training, but they might look like this:

```
tech
Cluster number:  2 number of items:  60
Cluster number:  4 number of items:  9
Cluster number:  3 number of items:  10
Cluster number:  1 number of items:  2
business
Cluster number:  3 number of items:  100
Cluster number:  0 number of items:  1
Cluster number:  2 number of items:  1
sport
Cluster number:  4 number of items:  98
Cluster number:  3 number of items:  5
entertainment
Cluster number:  1 number of items:  45
Cluster number:  3 number of items:  32
Cluster number:  4 number of items:  1
politics
Cluster number:  0 number of items:  59
Cluster number:  3 number of items:  24
Cluster number:  4 number of items:  1
```

12. The `print_most_common_words_by_cluster` function will print out the top 200 words for each cluster:

```
def print_most_common_words_by_cluster(all_training, km,
num_clusters):
    clusters = km.labels_.tolist()
    docs = {'text': all_training, 'cluster': clusters}
```

```
frame = pd.DataFrame(docs, index = [clusters])
for cluster in range(0, num_clusters):
    this_cluster_text = \
    frame[frame['cluster'] == cluster]
    all_text = \
    " ".join(this_cluster_text['text'].astype(str))
    top_200 = get_most_frequent_words(all_text)
    print(cluster)
    print(top_200)
return frame
```

13. Using `print_most_common_words_by_cluster`, we can see which cluster is which:

```
print_most_common_words_by_cluster(all_training, km)
```

The results will vary from run to run but might look like this:

```
0
```

```
['people', 'technology', 'music', 'mobile', 'users',
'new', 'use', 'net', 'digital', 'software', 'phone',
'make', 'service', 'year', 'used', 'broadband', 'uk',
'online', 'computer', 'get', 'services', 'security',
'information', 'phones', 'using', 'data', 'internet',
'microsoft', 'tv', 'system', 'million', 'first', 'world',
'video', 'work', 'content', 'search', 'access', 'number',
'networks', 'says', 'time', 'firm', 'web', 'apple',
'research', 'firms', 'industry', 'media', 'sites',
'devices', 'site', 'network', 'home', 'help', 'last',
'market', …]
```

```
1
```

```
['game', 'games', 'first', 'england', 'world', 'win',
'time', 'last', 'play', 'players', 'new', 'back',
'year', 'get', 'cup', 'good', 'm', 'wales', 'o', 'side',
'team', 'ireland', 'six', 'match', 'set', 'final',
'won', 'three', 'next', 'club', 'season', 'added',
'take', 'playing', 'rugby', 'coach', 'years', 'france',
'best', 'player', 'make', 'chelsea', 'injury', 'victory',
'think', 'played', 'great', 'minutes', 'start', 'told',
'nations', 'people', 'come', 'league', 'week', 'title',
'open', 'top', 'try', 'end', 'arsenal', 'scotland',
'international', 'chance', 'five', …]
```

```
2
```

```
['year', 'new', 'government', 'last', 'company',
'people', 'market', 'years', 'uk', 'world', 'sales',
'firm', 'growth', 'economy', 'first', 'bank', 'group',
'told', 'three', 'time', 'oil', 'deal', 'economic',
'china', 'shares', 'number', 'chief', 'business', 'make',
'show', 'law', 'added', 'expected', 'prices', 'country',
'music', 'companies', 'public', 'european', 'next',
'london', 'rise', 'financial', 'million', 'money',
'countries', 'bbc', 'executive', 'work', 'part', 'back',
'months', 'firms', 'says', 'week', 'news', 'set', 'take',
'foreign', 'top', 'figures', 'say', 'home', ...]
```

```
3
```

```
['film', 'best', 'awards', 'year', 'award', 'films',
'director', 'won', 'actor', 'new', 'star', 'actress',
'british', 'first', 'years', 'last', 'tv', 'show',
'festival', 'comedy', 'people', 'uk', 'movie', 'oscar',
'bbc', 'role', 'hollywood', 'aviator', 'prize',
'music', 'song', 'three', 'including', 'stars', 'time',
'top', 'nominations', 'world', 'nominated', 'million',
'ceremony', 'office', 'oscars', 'win', 'drama', 'number',
'category', 'starring', 'box', 'academy', 'book',
'london', 'life', 'named', 'series', 'theatre', 'love',
'think', 'make', 'musical', 'took', 'baby', 'play', ...]
```

```
4
```

```
['labour', 'blair', 'election', 'party', 'government',
'people', 'minister', 'howard', 'brown', 'prime', 'tory',
'new', 'told', 'plans', 'leader', 'public', 'tories',
'tax', 'say', 'chancellor', 'britain', 'tony', 'general',
'campaign', 'bbc', 'next', 'secretary', 'uk', 'says',
'michael', 'lib', 'lord', 'kennedy', 'country', 'get',
'home', 'time', 'make', 'liberal', 'last', 'political',
'issue', 'parties', 'mps', 'vote', 'year', 'ukip',
'first', 'conservative', 'voters', 'added', 'house',
'british', 'take', 'spokesman', 'think', 'saying',
'back', 'bill', 'believe', 'years', 'politics', ...]
```

14. We will now save our model. Import the `pickle` package:

```
import pickle
```

15. We will now create the vectorizer and get the vector matrix for the training data:

```
pickle.dump(km, open("bbc_kmeans.pkl", "wb"))
```

16. You can later load the model as follows:

```
km = pickle.load(open("bbc_kmeans.pkl", "rb"))
```

How it works...

In *step 1*, we import the necessary packages and functions. In *step 2*, we initialize the global variables, including the stopwords and the Snowball stemmer object we will use.

In *step 3*, we get the BBC data as a dictionary by topic and then divide it into training and testing data. In *step 4*, we create text lists for all the training and test data. In *step 5*, we define the `tokenize_and_stem` function we will use. This function tokenizes the input text into words, filters out punctuation and non-letter-containing words, and stems them.

In *step 6*, we define the `create_vectorizer` function. This function creates a TF-IDF vectorizer that considers uni-, bi-, and trigrams. In *step 7*, we create the vectorizer using the training data and then transform the training text to get the vector matrix.

In *step 8*, we create and fit the `KMeans` classifier. We initialize it with five as the number of clusters, as that is the number of topics in our data. When you do your own projects on unlabeled data, you will have to guess the number of clusters. In his book *The Hundred Page Machine Learning Book*, Andriy Burkov describes an algorithm to determine the number of clusters most likely present in your model. The `init` argument is the way the classifier initializes its clusters, and the `random_state` argument makes sure that the random state generated by the model is deterministic. After initializing the classifier, we fit the classifier on the training data matrix.

In *step 9*, we define the `make_predictions` function, which will return a list of cluster numbers for input data. Since the input data needs to be vectorized, the function takes in the data, the vectorizer, and the `KMeans` classifier.

In *step 10*, we define the `print_report` function, which prints out statistics about the model. It takes in the data dictionary that includes the topic information. It then prints out the number of items per cluster for each topic.

In *step 11*, we use the `make_predictions` function to use the model on unseen data and then print out the statistics using the `print_report` function. As we see, all topics have more than one cluster as assigned results, which means that the accuracy is not 100%. The topics that have the best results, or the most texts in one cluster, are business and sport, which are also the topics with the largest number of examples.

The `print_report` function takes the test data and prints the number of texts in each topic that were classified in each numbered cluster.

In *step 12*, we define `print_most_common_words_by_cluster`. This takes the texts for each cluster and creates a `FreqDist` object based on those texts, before printing the top 200 most frequent words in each cluster.

In *step 13*, we use the `print_most_common_words_by_cluster` function on the training data. Looking at those results, we can conclude that `cluster 0` is `tech`, `cluster 1` is `sport`, `cluster 2` is `business`, `cluster 3` is `entertainment`, and `cluster 4` is `politics`.

In *step 14*, we import the `pickle` package, which will enable us to save the model. In *step 15*, we save the model to a file on disk. *Step 16* shows how to later load the model for further use.

Using SVMs for supervised text classification

In this recipe, we will build a machine learning classifier that uses the SVM algorithm. By the end of the recipe, you will have a working classifier that you will be able to test on new inputs and evaluate using the same `classification_report` tools as we used in the previous sections.

Getting ready

We will continue working with the same packages that we already installed in the previous recipes.

How to do it...

We will start with the already familiar steps of dividing data into training and testing sets and creating a vectorizer. We will then train the SVM classifier and evaluate it.

Your steps are as follows:

1. Import the necessary functions and packages:

```
import numpy as np
import pandas as pd
import string
import pickle
from sklearn import svm
from sklearn import preprocessing
from sklearn.metrics import classification_report
from sklearn.model_selection import train_test_split
```

```
from sklearn.feature_extraction.text import
TfidfVectorizer
from Chapter01.tokenization import tokenize_nltk
from Chapter04.unsupervised_text_classification import
tokenize_and_stem
from Chapter04.preprocess_bbc_dataset import get_data
from Chapter04.keyword_classification import get_labels
from Chapter04.preprocess_bbc_dataset import get_
stopwords
```

2. Initialize the global variables:

```
bbc_dataset = "Chapter04/bbc-text.csv"
stopwords_file_path = "Chapter01/stopwords.csv"
stopwords = get_stopwords(stopwords_file_path)
```

3. Get the data and create a `LabelEncoder` object:

```
data_dict = get_data(bbc_dataset)
le = get_labels(list(data_dict.keys()))
```

4. The `create_dataset` function will take the data dictionary and create a `pandas` `DataFrame` object with the data:

```
def create_dataset(data_dict, le):
    text = []
    labels = []
    for topic in data_dict:
        label = le.transform([topic])
        text = text + data_dict[topic]
        this_topic_labels = \
        [label[0]]*len(data_dict[topic])
        labels = labels + this_topic_labels
    docs = {'text':text, 'label':labels}
    frame = pd.DataFrame(docs)
    return frame
```

5. The `split_dataset` function splits the DataFrame into training and test sets:

```
def split_dataset(df, train_column_name,
                     gold_column_name, test_percent):
    X_train, X_test, y_train, y_test = \
    train_test_split(df[train_column_name],
                        df[gold_column_name],
                        test_size=test_percent,
                        random_state=0)
    return (X_train, X_test, y_train, y_test)
```

6. The `create_and_fit_vectorizer` function will create and fit the vectorizer on the provided data:

```
def create_and_fit_vectorizer(training_text):
    vec = \
    TfidfVectorizer(max_df=0.90, min_df=0.05,
                       stop_words=stopwords, use_idf=True,
                       tokenizer=tokenize_and_stem,
                       ngram_range=(1,3))
    return vec.fit(training_text)
```

7. Using the data dictionary and the functions previously defined, we will create the test and training data:

```
df = create_dataset(data_dict, le)
(X_train, X_test, y_train, y_test) = \
split_dataset(df, 'text', 'label')
vectorizer = create_and_fit_vectorizer(X_train)
X_train = vectorizer.transform(X_train).todense()
X_test = vectorizer.transform(X_test).todense()
```

8. The `train_svm_classifier` function takes the data and returns a trained SVM classifier:

```
def train_svm_classifier(X_train, y_train):
    clf = svm.SVC(C=1, kernel='linear',
                     decision_function_shape='ovo')
    clf = clf.fit(X_train, y_train)
    return clf
```

9. The `evaluate` function prints out a statistics report:

```
def evaluate(clf, X_test, y_test, le):
    y_pred = clf.predict(X_test)
    print(classification_report(y_test, y_pred,
        labels=le.transform(le.classes_),
        target_names=le.classes_))
```

10. Using the preceding functions, we will train the classifier, save it, and then evaluate it:

```
clf = train_svm_classifier(X_train, y_train)
pickle.dump(clf, open("Chapter04/bbc_svm.pkl", "wb"))
evaluate(clf, X_test, y_test, le)
```

The result will be as follows:

	precision	recall	f1-score	support
business	0.93	0.93	0.93	105
entertainment	0.96	0.96	0.96	78
politics	0.93	0.94	0.94	72
sport	0.98	0.99	0.99	106
tech	0.96	0.94	0.95	84
accuracy			0.96	445
macro avg	0.95	0.95	0.95	445
weighted avg	0.96	0.96	0.96	445

11. The `test_new_example` function will take in a string, the classifier, the vectorizer, and the label encoder and provide a prediction:

```
def test_new_example(input_string, clf, vectorizer, le):
    vector = \
    vectorizer.transform([input_string]).todense()
    prediction = clf.predict(vector)
    print(prediction)
    label = le.inverse_transform(prediction)
    print(label)
```

12. We will test the preceding function on a new article:

```
new_example = """iPhone 12: Apple makes jump to 5G
Apple has confirmed its iPhone 12 handsets will be its
first to work on faster 5G networks.
The company has also extended the range to include a new
"Mini" model that has a smaller 5.4in screen.
The US firm bucked a wider industry downturn by
increasing its handset sales over the past year.
But some experts say the new features give Apple its best
opportunity for growth since 2014, when it revamped its
line-up with the iPhone 6.
"5G will bring a new level of performance for downloads
and uploads, higher quality video streaming, more
responsive gaming, real-time interactivity and so much
more," said chief executive Tim Cook.
..."""

test_new_example(new_example, clf, vectorizer, le)
```

The result will be as follows:

```
[4]
['tech']
```

How it works...

In *step 1*, we import the necessary functions and packages. In *step 2*, we initialize the global variables. In *step 3*, we get the data dictionary using the `get_data` function from the *Getting the dataset and evaluation baseline ready* recipe in this chapter. Then we create a label encoder object using the `get_labels` function from the *Performing rule-based text classification using keywords* recipe in this chapter.

In *step 4*, we define the `create_dataset` function, which takes in the data dictionary and creates a `pandas` `DataFrame` object. The `text` column in this DataFrame contains the text in the dataset, and the `label` column contains the transformed label assigned to the item.

In *step 5*, we define the `split_dataset` function, which splits the DataFrame into test and training sets. It takes in as arguments the DataFrame, the name of the column that contains the text to be trained on, the name of the column that contains the label, and the proportion of data to be used as test data. It then uses the `sklearn train_test_split` function and returns four `numpy` arrays: two arrays with data, one for testing and one for training (`X_test` and `X_train`), and two arrays with labels, one for testing and one for training (`y_test` and `y_train`).

In *step 6*, we define the `create_and_fit_vectorizer` function, which creates a TFIDF vectorizer that encodes uni-, bi-, and trigrams. It returns the vectorizer fitted on the training data.

In *step 7*, we use the functions defined in *steps 4* to *6*. First, we create the dataset as a DataFrame using the `create_dataset` function. Then we divide the dataset into testing and training using the `split_dataset` function, leaving 20% of the data for testing. We create the vectorizer using the `create_and_fit_vectorizer` function, using just the training data for it. Finally, we transform the training and test data using the vectorizer.

In *step 8*, we define the `train_svm_classifier` function. It trains an SVM classifier with the regularization parameter of `1` and the linear kernel. The regularization parameter serves to reduce overfitting in machine learning models. You can experiment with different values for it. There are different kernels that are used by the SVM algorithm, which are different ways to separate data into its classes. The linear kernel is the simplest one.

In *step 9*, we define the `evaluate` function. It compares the labels provided in the dataset with the classifier predictions and prints out the classification report with accuracy, precision, and recall information for the model.

In *step 10*, we use the train the SVM classifier, save it to a file using the `pickle` package and then evaluate it. We achieve an accuracy of 96%.

In *step 11*, we define the `test_new_example` function, which will take in a text and classify it using our model. It takes the input string, classifier, vectorizer, and label encoder. It transforms the input text using the vectorizer, gets a prediction from the model, and then decodes the prediction into a text label.

In *step 12*, we use the `test_new_example` function to make a prediction on a tech article. We see that the prediction is indeed `tech`.

There's more...

There are many different machine learning algorithms that can be used instead of the SVM algorithm. Some of the others are regression, Naïve Bayes, and decision trees. You can experiment with them and see which ones perform better.

Using LSTMs for supervised text classification

In this recipe, we will build a deep learning LSTM classifier for the BBC News dataset. There is not enough data to build a great classifier, but we will use the same dataset for comparison. By the end of this recipe, you will have a complete LSTM classifier that is trained and can be tested on new inputs.

Getting ready

In order to build the recipe, we need to install `tensorflow` and `keras`:

```
pip install tensorflow
pip install keras
```

In this recipe, we will use the same BBC dataset to create an LSTM classification model.

How to do it...

The general structure of the training is similar to plain machine learning model training, where we clean the data, create the dataset, and split it into training and testing datasets. We then train a model and test it on unseen data. The particulars of the training are different for deep learning as opposed to statistical machine learning, such as SVMs. The steps for this recipe are as follows:

1. Import the necessary functions and packages:

```
import pandas as pd
import numpy as np
from keras.preprocessing.text import Tokenizer
from keras.preprocessing.sequence import pad_sequences
from sklearn.model_selection import train_test_split
from sklearn.metrics import classification_report
import tensorflow as tf
from keras import Sequential
from tensorflow.keras.layers import Embedding
```

```
from tensorflow.keras.layers import SpatialDropout1D
from tensorflow.keras.layers import LSTM
from tensorflow.keras.layers import Dense
from tensorflow.keras.callbacks import EarlyStopping
from keras.models import load_model
import matplotlib.pyplot as plt
from Chapter04.preprocess_bbc_dataset import get_data
from Chapter04.keyword_classification import get_labels
from Chapter04.preprocess_bbc_dataset import get_
stopwords
from Chapter04.svm_classification import create_dataset,
new_example
```

2. Initialize the global variables:

```
MAX_NUM_WORDS = 50000
MAX_SEQUENCE_LENGTH = 1000
EMBEDDING_DIM = 300
bbc_dataset = "Chapter04/bbc-text.csv"
```

3. The `create_tokenizer` function creates a tokenizer for the LSTM model:

```
def create_tokenizer(input_data, save_path):
    tokenizer = \
    Tokenizer(num_words=MAX_NUM_WORDS,
            filters='!"#$%&()*+,-./:;<=>?@[\]^_`{|}~',
            lower=True)
    tokenizer.fit_on_texts(input_data)
    save_tokenizer(tokenizer, save_path)
    return tokenizer
```

4. The `save_tokenizer` and `load_tokenizer` functions save and load tokenizers:

```
def save_tokenizer(tokenizer, filename):
    with open(filename, 'wb') as f:
        pickle.dump(tokenizer, f,
                protocol=pickle.HIGHEST_PROTOCOL)
```

```
def load_tokenizer(filename):
    with open('tokenizer.pickle', 'rb') as f:
        tokenizer = pickle.load(f)
    return tokenizer
```

5. The `plot_model` function takes a history object from a trained model and plots the model's loss for testing and training data, which helps to evaluate the training process:

```
def plot_model(history):
    plt.title('Loss')
    plt.plot(history.history['loss'], label='train')
    plt.plot(history.history['val_loss'],
             label='test')
    plt.legend()
    plt.show()
```

6. The `evaluate_model` function prints out the already familiar classification report:

```
def evaluate(model, X_test, Y_test, le):
    Y_pred = model.predict(X_test)
    Y_pred = Y_pred.argmax(axis=-1)
    Y_test = Y_test.argmax(axis=-1)
    Y_new_pred = [le.inverse_transform([value]) for
                  value in Y_pred]
    Y_new_test = [le.inverse_transform([value]) for
                  value in Y_test]
    print(classification_report(Y_new_test,
                                Y_new_pred))
```

7. The `train_model` function takes the input DataFrame and a `LabelEncoder` object as input, trains an LSTM model, saves it, evaluates it, and plots its loss:

```
def train_model(df, le):
    tokenizer = \
    create_tokenizer(df['text'].values,
                     'Chapter04/bbc_tokenizer.pickle')
    X = transform_text(tokenizer, df['text'].values)
```

```
Y = pd.get_dummies(df['label']).values
X_train, X_test, Y_train, Y_test = \
train_test_split(X,Y, test_size = 0.20,
                 random_state = 42)
model = Sequential()
optimizer = tf.keras.optimizers.Adam(0.0001)
model.add(Embedding(MAX_NB_WORDS, EMBEDDING_DIM,
                    input_length=X.shape[1]))
model.add(SpatialDropout1D(0.2))
model.add(LSTM(100, dropout=0.2,
               recurrent_dropout=0.2))
model.add(Dense(5, activation='softmax'))
#Standard for multiclass classification
loss='categorical_crossentropy'
model.compile(loss=loss, optimizer=optimizer,
              metrics=['accuracy'])
epochs = 7
batch_size = 64
es = EarlyStopping(monitor='val_loss', patience=3,
                   min_delta=0.0001)
history = model.fit(X_train, Y_train,
                    epochs=epochs,
                    batch_size=batch_size,
                    validation_split=0.2,
                    callbacks=[es])
accr = model.evaluate(X_test,Y_test)
print('Test set\n  Loss: {:0.3f}\n  Accuracy: \
      {:0.3f}'.format(accr[0],accr[1]))
model.save('Chapter04/bbc_model_scratch1.h5')
evaluate(model, X_test, Y_test, le)
plot_model(history)
```

8. Let's load the data, create a label encoder, and create the dataset:

```
data_dict = get_data(bbc_dataset)
le = get_labels(list(data_dict.keys()))
df = create_dataset(data_dict, le)
```

9. Now we can train the model using the `train_model` function defined previously:

```
train_model(df, le)
```

The output will vary, but here is an example:

```
Epoch 1/7
23/23 [==============================] - 279s 12s/step -
loss: 1.5695 - accuracy: 0.3083 - val_loss: 1.4268 - val_
accuracy: 0.3596

...

Epoch 7/7
23/23 [==============================] - 259s 11s/step -
loss: 0.0402 - accuracy: 0.9944 - val_loss: 0.5588 - val_
accuracy: 0.8258
14/14 [==============================] - 10s 732ms/step -
loss: 0.4948 - accuracy: 0.8427
Test set
   Loss: 0.495
   Accuracy: 0.843
```

	precision	recall	f1-score	support
business	0.87	0.94	0.90	104
entertainment	0.82	0.73	0.77	75
politics	0.81	0.73	0.77	82
sport	0.97	0.85	0.90	99
tech	0.75	0.92	0.83	85
accuracy			0.84	445
macro avg	0.84	0.83	0.84	445
weighted avg	0.85	0.84	0.84	445

And the plot of the loss function might look like this:

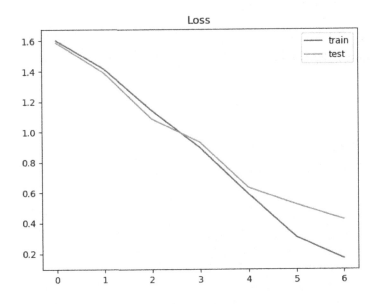

Figure 4.1 – Plot of the training and test loss function

10. We will have a function to load and test an existing model:

```
def load_and_evaluate_existing_model(model_path,
tokenizer_path, df, le):
    model = load_model(model_path)
    tokenizer = load_tokenizer(tokenizer_path)
    X = transform_text(tokenizer, df['text'].values)
    Y = pd.get_dummies(df['label']).values
    evaluate(model, X, Y, le)
```

11. The `test_new_example` function will take in a string, the classifier, the vectorizer, and the label encoder and provide a prediction:

```
def test_new_example(model, tokenizer, le, text_input):
    X_example = transform_text(tokenizer, new_example)
    label_array = model.predict(X_example)
    new_label = np.argmax(label_array, axis=-1)
    print(new_label)
    print(le.inverse_transform(new_label))
```

12. We will test the preceding function on the same tech article as we did in the *Using SVMs for supervised text classification* recipe:

```
test_new_example(model, tokenizer, le, new_example)
```

The result will be as follows:

```
[4]
```
```
['tech']
```

How it works...

In *step 1*, we import the packages and functions that we will need in this recipe.

In *step 2*, we initialize the global variables. The MAX_NUM_WORDS variable will have the maximum number of words that the tokenizer processes. The MAX_SEQUENCE_LENGTH variable is also used by the tokenizer and is the length of each input string that is fed into the model. Deep learning models require that each input string be of the same length, and that length is set in the MAX_SEQUENCE_LENGTH variable. The EMBEDDING_DIM variable sets the number of values to be used in the embedding vectors. Embedding vectors are similar to word2vec vectors, which encode each input text sequence.

In *step 3*, we define the create_tokenizer function, which creates the tokenizer required for LSTM. The tokenizer uses a set number of words for the model, which is set in the MAX_NUM_WORDS variable. It filters all punctuation, which is set in the filters parameter. It also lowercases all words. The function fits the tokenizer on the input data and then saves it to the provided path.

In *step 4*, we define the save_tokenizer and load_tokenizer functions to be used when loading pretrained models.

In *step 5*, we define the plot_model function. It takes the model history object and plots the training and validation loss, which is a useful tool in evaluating model performance.

> **Important note**
> Plotting the loss of a deep learning model is a useful tool in evaluating model performance. See this blog post to learn more about different possibilities: https://machinelearningmastery.com/learning-curves-for-diagnosing-machine-learning-model-performance/.

In *step 6*, we define the evaluate_model function, which should be familiar, as it prints out the classification report that we used in previous recipes.

In *step 7*, we define the `train_model` function. It creates a new model and then trains it. First, it uses the `create_tokenizer` function to get the tokenizer. It then uses the `transform_text` function to get the data into vector form. The `pad_sequences` function then adds empty values to each vector that is not the maximum size, so that all vectors are equal in length. We then one-hot encode the labels by using the pandas `get_dummies` function. After that, we split the dataset into training and testing parts. We then create a `Sequential` model and add layers to it. We use the Adam optimizer with a learning rate of 0.001. The first layer in the model is the embedding layer, the same type of embedding as used in the *Using word embeddings* recipe in *Chapter 3, Representing Text: Capturing Semantics*. We add the spatial dropout and the LSTM layers, followed by the dense layer. We then set the loss function to be categorical cross-entropy, which is standard for multi-class classification problems. We use seven epochs, or training rounds, and set 64 as the batch size. We use early stopping to prevent overfitting. We then train the model, save it, evaluate it, and plot its loss.

In *step 8*, we load the data, create a label encoder, and create the DataFrame with the input text. In *step 9*, we train the model using the `train_model` function and the input data. The accuracy on this dataset is not as good as with other methods: 84%. This is most likely because of the small amount of data for a deep learning network. This is corroborated by the loss plot, where the validation loss starts to deviate upward from the training loss, which happens frequently in situations with not enough data.

In *step 10*, we define the `load_and_evaluate_existing_model` function. Using this function, we can load and test an existing model on new data. In the function, we load the model and the tokenizer, transform the inputs, and evaluate them using the classification report.

In *step 11*, we define the `test_new_example` function. We load both the model and the tokenizer, apply the tokenizer to the text, and use the model on the transformed input. The output will be an array of probabilities for each class, so we have to transform it using the NumPy `argmax` function. This will get the most probable classification according to the model. After using the label encoder, we get the same `tech` label as before.

5

Getting Started with Information Extraction

In this chapter, we will cover the basics of information extraction. We will start with extracting emails and URLs from job announcements. Then we will use an algorithm called the **Levenshtein distance** to find similar strings. Next, we will use spaCy to find named entities in text, and later we will train our own **named entity recognition (NER)** model in spaCy. We will then do basic sentiment analysis, and finally, we will train two custom sentiment analysis models.

You will learn how to use existing tools and train your own models for information extraction tasks.

We will cover the following recipes in this chapter:

- Using regular expressions
- Finding similar strings: the Levenshtein distance
- Performing NER using spaCy
- Training your own NER model with spaCy

- Discovering sentiment analysis
- Sentiment for short texts using LSTM: Twitter
- Using BERT for sentiment analysis

Technical requirements

The code for this chapter is located in a folder named `Chapter05` in the GitHub repository of the book (`https://github.com/PacktPublishing/Python-Natural-Language-Processing-Cookbook`). In this chapter, you will need to install some additional packages using these commands:

```
pip install pandas
pip install python-Levenshtein
pip install spacy
pip install nltk
pip install textblob
pip install tqdm
pip install transformers
```

We will also need an additional package to segment Twitter hashtags, which can be downloaded at `https://github.com/jchook/wordseg`. After downloading, install it using this command:

```
python setup.py install
```

Using regular expressions

In this recipe, we will use regular expressions to find email addresses and URLs in text. Regular expressions are special character sequences that define search patterns. We will use a job descriptions dataset and write two regular expressions, one for emails and one for URLs.

Getting ready

We will need the `pandas` package for handling the data. If you haven't already installed it, install it like so:

```
pip install pandas
```

Download the job descriptions dataset from `https://www.kaggle.com/ andrewmvd/data-scientist-jobs`.

Here is a very handy tool for debugging regular expressions: `https://regex101. com/`. You can input a regular expression and a test string. It will show matches resulting from the regular expression, and the steps that the regular expression engine took in the process.

How to do it...

We will read the data from the CSV file into a pandas DataFrame and will use the Python `re` package to create regular expressions and search the text. The steps for this recipe are as follows:

1. Import the `re` and `pandas` packages and define the `data_file` variable:

```
import re
import pandas as pddata_file = "Chapter05/DataScientist.
csv"
```

2. The `get_items` functions will search a specific column in the DataFrame and find everything that matches the regular expression that is passed in:

```
def get_items(df, regex, column_name):
    df[column_name] = df['Job Description'].apply(
                        lambda x: re.findall(regex, x))
    return df
```

3. The `get_list_of_items` helper function takes a DataFrame as input and turns one of its columns into a list:

```
def get_list_of_items(df, column_name):
    items = []
    for index, row in df.iterrows():
        if (len(row[column_name]) > 0):
            for item in list(row[column_name]):
                if (type(item) is tuple and \
                len(item) > 1):
                    item = item[0]
```

```
                if (item not in items):
        items.append(item)
        return items
```

4. The `get_emails` function finds all emails in a DataFrame and returns them as a list:

```
def get_emails(df):
    email_regex='[^\s:|()\']+@[a-zA-Z0-9\.]+\.[a-zA-Z]+'
    df['emails'] = df['Job Description'].apply(
                lambda x: re.findall(email_regex, x))
    emails = get_list_of_items(df, 'emails')
    return emails
```

5. The `get_urls` helper function takes a DataFrame as input and turns one of its columns into a list:

```
def get_urls(df):
    url_regex = '(http[s]?://(www\.)?[A-Za-z0-9-_\.\-]+\.
[A-Za-z]+/?[A-Za-z0-9$\-_\-\/\.\?]*)[\.)\"]*'
    df = get_items(df, url_regex, 'urls')
    urls = get_list_of_items(df, 'urls')
    return urls
```

6. Now we will read the CSV file into a DataFrame using the pandas `read_csv` method:

```
df = pd.read_csv(data_file, encoding='utf-8')
```

7. We will now get the emails:

```
emails = get_emails(df)
print(emails)
```

Part of the result will look like this:

```
['security@quartethealth.com', 'talent@quartethealth.
com', 'accommodations-ext@fb.com', 'talent@ebay.com',
'recruiting-inquiries@deshaw.com', 'cvwithdraw@deshaw.
com', 'backgroundcheck-inquiries@deshaw.com', 'Candidate.
Accommodations@Disney.com', 'careers@springhealth.com',
'TalentAcquisition@grubhub.com', 'privacy@grubhub.com',
'jobs@temboo.com', 'careers@Healthfirst.org', 'mailbox_
tas_recruit@humana.com', …]
```

8. We will get the URLs in a similar fashion:

```
urls = get_urls(df)
print(urls)
```

Part of the result will look like this:

```
['https://www.decode-m.com/', 'https://www.amazon.jobs/
en/disability/us.', 'https://www.techatbloomberg.com/
nlp/', 'https://bloomberg.com/company/d4gx/', 'https://
www.dol.gov/ofccp/regs/compliance/posters/ofccpost.
htm', 'http://www.tapestry.com/', 'https://www.arena.
io/about/careers.html', 'http://www.fujitsu.com/global/
about/corporate/info/', 'http://www.fujitsu.com/global/
digitalannealer/', 'http://www.fujitsu.com/global/
solutions/business-technology/ai/', …]
```

How it works...

Now let's look at how the steps from the preceding section work.

In *step 1*, we import re and pandas, the two packages that we need, and define the path to the dataset.

In *step 2*, we define the get_items function, which takes a DataFrame, a regular expression, and a column name, and creates a new column that contains the search results. The function applies the regular expression to every entry in the Job Description column and stores the results in the new column.

In *step 3*, we define the get_list_of_items function, which takes in a DataFrame and returns a list of found items in the specified column. This function also removes duplicates and only leaves the match parts that are necessary (that appear first in this case). In the case of URLs, we match using groups, and the re package returns a tuple of results that include all groups matched. We use just the first group that is the actual URL match.

In *step 4*, we define the `get_emails` function to get all the emails that appear in the `Job Description` column. The regular expression consists of three parts that appear in square brackets followed by quantifiers:

- `[^\s:|()\']` + is the username part of the regular expression, followed by the @ sign. It consists of one group of characters, which is shown in square brackets. Any characters from this group may appear in the username one or more times. This is shown using the + quantifier. The characters in the username can be anything but a space (`\s`), colon, |, or an apostrophe. The ^ character shows the negation of the character class. The apostrophe is a special character in regular expressions and has to be escaped with a backward slash in order to invoke the regular meaning of the character.

- `[a-zA-Z0-9\.]` + is the first part of the domain name, followed by a dot. This part is simply alphanumeric characters, lower or upper case, and a dot appearing one or more times. Since a dot is a special character, we escape it with a backward slash. The `a-z` expression signifies a range of characters from a to z.

- `[a-zA-Z]` + is the last part of the domain name, which is the top-level domain, such as .com, .org, and so on. Usually, no digits are allowed in these top-level domains, and the regular expression matches lower or upper characters that appear one or more times.

This regular expression is sufficient to parse all emails in the dataset and not present any false positives. You might find that in your data there are additional adjustments that need to be made to the regular expression.

In *step 5*, we define the `get_urls` function that returns all URLs in a specified Data Frame. URLs are significantly more complicated than emails, and here is a breakdown of the regular expression:

- `http[s]?://`: This is the `http` part of the URL. All URLs in this dataset had this part; that might not be the case in your data, and you will have to adjust the regular expression accordingly. This part of the expression will match both `http` and `https`, since s is listed as appearing zero times or once, which is signified by the ? quantifier.

- `(www\.)?`: Next, we have a group of characters, which are treated as a unit, but they all have to appear in the order they are listed. In this case, this is the www part of the URL followed by a dot, escaped with a backward slash. The group of characters may appear zero times or once, signified by the ? character at the end.

- `[A-Za-z0-9-_\.\-]+`: This part is the domain name of the website, followed by the top-level domain. Website names also include dashes, and the dot character appears before the top-level domain and subdomains.

- `/?[A-Za-z0-9$\-_\-\/\.\?]*)`: This last part is whatever follows the domain name after the slash. It could be a variety of characters that list files, parameters, and so on. They could or could not be present, and that is why they are followed by the `*` quantifier. The bracket at the end signifies the end of the matching group.

- `[\.)\"]*`: Many URLs in this dataset are followed by dots, brackets, and other characters, and this is the last part of the regular expression.

In *step 6*, we read the dataset into a pandas DataFrame. In *step 7*, we use the `get_emails` function to parse all the emails out to the job description field. In *step 8*, we get the URLs using the `get_urls` function.

There's more...

Writing regular expressions can quickly turn into a messy affair. We use regular expression testing websites to enter the text that we expect a match and the regular expression. One example of such a site is `https://regex101.com/`.

Finding similar strings: the Levenshtein distance

When doing information extraction, in many cases we deal with misspellings, which can bring complications into the task. In order to get around this problem, several methods are available, including the Levenshtein distance. This algorithm finds the number of edits/additions/deletions needed to change one string into another. In this recipe, you will be able to use this technique to find a match for a misspelled email.

Getting ready

We will use the same packages and the dataset that we used in the previous recipe, and also the `python-Levenshtein` package, which can be installed using the following command:

```
pip install python-Levenshtein
```

How to do it...

We will read the dataset into a pandas DataFrame and use the emails extracted from it to search for a misspelled email.

Your steps should be formatted like so:

1. Do the necessary imports:

    ```
    import pandas as pd
    import Levenshtein
    from Chapter05.regex import get_emails
    ```

2. Initialize the `data_file` variable:

    ```
    data_file = "Chapter05/DataScientist.csv"
    ```

3. The `find_levenshtein` function takes in a DataFrame and an input string and computes the Levenshtein distance between it and each string in the `email` column:

    ```
    def find_levenshtein(input_string, df):
        df['distance_to_' + input_string] = \
        df['emails'].apply(lambda x:Levenshtein.distance(
                                          input_string, x))
        return df
    ```

4. The `get_closest_email_lev` function uses the function we defined in the previous step to find the email address that is closest to the one input:

    ```
    def get_closest_email_lev(df, email):
        df = find_levenshtein(email, df)
        column_name = 'distance_to_' + email
        minimum_value_email_index = df[column_name].idxmin()
        email = \
        df.loc[minimum_value_email_index]['emails']
        return email
    ```

5. Now we can read in the job descriptions DataFrame we used in the previous recipe and create a new DataFrame just from the emails:

```
df = pd.read_csv(data_file, encoding='utf-8')
emails = get_emails(df)
new_df = pd.DataFrame(emails,columns=['emails'])
```

6. Next, we use the misspelled email `rohitt.macdonald@prelim.com`to find a match in the new email DataFrame:

```
input_string = "rohitt.macdonald@prelim.com"
email = get_closest_email_lev(new_df, input_string)
print(email)
```

The output is as follows:

```
rohit.mcdonald@prolim.com
```

How it works...

In *step 1*, we import the `pandas` and the `Levenshtein` packages, as well as the `get_emails` function from the previous recipe.

In *step 2*, we define the path to the file with the dataset.

In *step 3*, we define the `find_levenshtein` function that takes in an input string and a DataFrame with emails and creates a new column where the value is the Levenshtein distance between the input and the email in the DataFrame. The column name is `distance_to_[input_string]`.

In *step 4*, we define the `get_closest_email_lev` function that takes in a DataFrame with emails and an email to match that returns the email in the DataFrame that is closest to the input. We accomplish this by using the `find_levenshtein` function to create a new column with distances to the input email and then using the `idxmin()` function from `pandas` to find the index of the minimum value. We use the minimum index to find the closest email.

In *step 5*, we read the dataset and get the emails, and then create a new DataFrame with just the emails.

In *step 6*, we define a misspelled email and use the `get_closest_email_lev` function to find the email that matches it, which is `rohit.mcdonald@prolim.com`, the correct spelling of the email.

There's more...

We can use another function, Jaro similarity, which outputs the similarity between two strings as a number between 0 and 1, where 1 means that two strings are the same. The process is similar, but we need the index with the maximum value instead of the minimum, since the Jaro similarity function returns a higher value for more similar strings. The steps are as follows:

1. The `find_jaro` function takes in a DataFrame and an input string and computes the Jaro similarity between it and each string in the `email` column:

```
def find_jaro(input_string, df):
    df['distance_to_' + input_string] = \
    df['emails'].apply(lambda x: Levenshtein.jaro(
                                    input_string, x))
    return df
```

2. The `get_closest_email_jaro` function uses the function we defined in the previous step to find the email address that is closest to the one input:

```
def get_closest_email_jaro(df, email):
    df = find_jaro(email, df)
    column_name = 'distance_to_' + email
    maximum_value_email_index = df[column_name].idxmax()
    email = \
    df.loc[maximum_value_email_index]['emails']
    return email
```

3. Now we can read in the job descriptions DataFrame we used in the previous recipe and create a new DataFrame just from the emails:

```
df = pd.read_csv(data_file, encoding='utf-8')
emails = get_emails(df)
new_df = pd.DataFrame(emails,columns=['emails'])
```

4. Next, we use the misspelled email `rohitt.macdonald@prelim.com` to find a match in the new email DataFrame:

```
input_string = "rohitt.macdonald@prelim.com"
email = get_closest_email_jaro(new_df, input_string)
print(email)
```

The output is as follows:

```
rohit.mcdonald@prolim.com
```

An extension of the Jaro similarity function is the Jaro-Winkler function, which attaches a weight to the end of the word, and that weight lowers the importance of misspellings toward the end, for example:

```
print(Levenshtein.jaro_winkler("rohit.mcdonald@prolim.com",
        "rohit.mcdonald@prolim.org"))
```

The resultant output would be as follows:

```
1.0
```

See also

There is another Python package that has string similarity functions, `jellyfish`. It has other features, such as converting a spelling into a phonetic string, which allows the matching of strings based on the way they sound, as well as fuzzy string matching, including Levenshtein and others.

Performing named entity recognition using spaCy

In this recipe, we will parse out named entities from an article text used in *Chapter 4, Classifying Texts*. We will load the package and the parsing engine, and loop through the NER results.

Getting ready

In this recipe, we will use the `spacy` package. If you haven't installed it yet, install it using the following command:

```
pip install spacy
```

After you install spaCy, you will need to download a language model. We will download the small model:

```
python -m spacy download en_core_web_sm
```

How to do it...

The NER happens automatically with the processing that spaCy does for an input text. Accessing the entities happens through the `doc.ents` variable. The steps for this recipe are as follows:

1. Import `spacy`:

```
import spacy
```

2. Initialize the spaCy engine:

```
nlp = spacy.load("en_core_web_sm")
```

3. Initialize the article text:

```
article = """iPhone 12: Apple makes jump to 5G

Apple has confirmed its iPhone 12 handsets will be its
first to work on faster 5G networks.

The company has also extended the range to include a new
"Mini" model that has a smaller 5.4in screen.

The US firm bucked a wider industry downturn by
increasing its handset sales over the past year.

But some experts say the new features give Apple its best
opportunity for growth since 2014, when it revamped its
line-up with the iPhone 6.

…

"Networks are going to have to offer eye-wateringly
attractive deals, and the way they're going to do that is
on great tariffs and attractive trade-in deals,"

predicted Ben Wood from the consultancy CCS Insight.
Apple typically unveils its new iPhones in September, but
opted for a later date this year.

It has not said why, but it was widely speculated to be
related to disruption caused by the coronavirus pandemic.
The firm's shares ended the day 2.7% lower.

This has been linked to reports that several Chinese
internet platforms opted not to carry the livestream,

although it was still widely viewed and commented on via
the social media network Sina Weibo."""
```

4. Create the spaCy Doc object:

```
doc = nlp(article)
```

5. Loop through the entities and print their information:

```
for ent in doc.ents:
    print(ent.text, ent.start_char, ent.end_char,
        ent.label_)
```

The result will be as follows:

```
12 7 9 CARDINAL
Apple 11 16 ORG
5 31 32 CARDINAL
Apple 34 39 ORG
iPhone 58 64 ORG
first 89 94 ORDINAL
5 113 114 CARDINAL
Mini 185 189 WORK_OF_ART
5.4 216 219 CARDINAL
...
the day 2586 2593 DATE
2.7% 2594 2598 PERCENT
Chinese 2652 2659 NORP
Sina Weibo 2797 2807 PERSON
```

How it works...

In *step 1*, we import the spacy package. In *step 2*, we load the small English model, and in *step 3*, we initialize the article text. In *step 4*, we process the article using the spaCy engine and create a Doc object.

In *step 5*, we loop through the named entities that are contained in the text and print out their information: the entity text, the index of the start character, the index of the end character, and the label of the named entity. The meaning of the labels can be found in the spaCy documentation at https://spacy.io/api/annotation#named-entities.

There's more...

You can experiment with different spaCy models. We downloaded the small spaCy language model, and the accuracy of the medium and large models might be higher. For example, you might download the medium model:

```
python -m spacy download en_core_web_md
```

And later load it in your program:

```
nlp = spacy.load("en_core_web_md")
```

After running the same code, but with a different model, you will notice that the output will be slightly different, and possibly better.

Training your own NER model with spaCy

The NER model provided by spaCy can suffice in many cases. There might be other times, however, when we would like to augment the existing model or create a new one from scratch. spaCy has a toolset specifically for that, and in this recipe, we will do both.

Getting ready

We will use the spacy package to train a new NER model. You do not need any other packages than spacy.

How to do it...

We will define our training data and then use it to update an existing model. We will then test the model and save it to disk. The code in this recipe is based on the spaCy documentation (https://spacy.io/usage/training#ner). The steps for this recipe are as follows:

1. Import the necessary packages:

```
import spacy
from spacy.util import minibatch, compounding
from spacy.language import Language
import warnings
import random
from pathlib import Path
```

2. Now we will define the training data that we will use:

```
DATA = [
    ("A fakir from far-away India travels to Asterix's\
    village and asks Cacofonix to save his land from\
    drought since his singing can cause rain.",
        {'entities':[(39, 46, "PERSON"),
                    (66, 75, "PERSON")]}),
    ("Cacofonix, accompanied by Asterix and Obelix,\
    must travel to India aboard a magic carpet to\
    save the life of the princess Orinjade, who is to\
    be sacrificed to stop the drought.",
        {'entities':[(0, 9, "PERSON"),
                    (26, 33, "PERSON"),
                    (38, 44, "PERSON"),
                    (61, 66, "LOC"),
                    (122, 130, "PERSON")]})
]
```

3. The N_ITER variable contains the number of training iterations and the OUTPUT_DIR variable lists the directory where the model should be saved:

```
N_ITER=100
OUTPUT_DIR = "Chapter05/model_output"
```

4. The save_model function saves the model to the specified directory:

```
def save_model(nlp, output_dir):
    output_dir = Path(output_dir)
    if not output_dir.exists():
        output_dir.mkdir()
    nlp.to_disk(output_dir)
```

5. The load_model function loads a model from the specified directory:

```
def load_model(input_dir):
    nlp = spacy.load(input_dir)
    return nlp
```

6. The `create_model` function either creates a new blank model or loads a model specified by the `model` argument:

```
def create_model(model):
    if (model is not None):
        nlp = spacy.load(model)
    else:
        nlp = spacy.blank("en")
    return nlp
```

7. The `add_ner_to_model` function adds the NER model to the spaCy pipeline:

```
def add_ner_to_model(nlp):
    if "ner" not in nlp.pipe_names:
        ner = nlp.create_pipe("ner")
        nlp.add_pipe(ner, last=True)
    else:
        ner = nlp.get_pipe("ner")
    return (nlp, ner)
```

8. In the `add_labels` function, we add the named entity labels that need to be recognized by the model:

```
def add_labels(ner, data):
    for sentence, annotations in data:
        for ent in annotations.get("entities"):
            ner.add_label(ent[2])
    return ner
```

9. Now we can define the `train_model` function:

```
def train_model(model=None):
    nlp = create_model(model)
    (nlp, ner) = add_ner_to_model(nlp)
    ner = add_labels(ner, DATA)
    pipe_exceptions = ["ner", "trf_wordpiecer",
                       "trf_tok2vec"]
    other_pipes = [pipe for pipe in nlp.pipe_names if
                   pipe not in pipe_exceptions]
    with nlp.disable_pipes(*other_pipes), \
```

```
    warnings.catch_warnings():
        warnings.filterwarnings("once",
                               category=UserWarning,
                               module='spacy')
    if model is None:
        nlp.begin_training()
    for itn in range(N_ITER):
        random.shuffle(DATA)
        losses = {}
        batches = minibatch(DATA,
                size=compounding(4.0, 32.0, 1.001))
        for batch in batches:
            texts, annotations = zip(*batch)
            nlp.update(
                texts,
                annotations,
                drop=0.5,
                losses=losses,
            )
        print("Losses", losses)
    return nlp
```

10. The `test_model` function will print the model output for a particular text:

```
def test_model(nlp, data):
    for text, annotations in data:
        doc = nlp(text)
        for ent in doc.ents:
            print(ent.text, ent.start_char, ent.end_char,
                ent.label_)
```

11. The `without_training` function will show us the output of the model before we do any training:

```
def without_training(data=DATA):
    nlp = spacy.load("en_core_web_sm")
    test_model(nlp, data)
```

12. Now we can put the code together. First, we output the entities that are output without any training:

```
without_training()
```

The output will be as follows:

```
India 22 27 GPE
Asterix 39 46 ORG
Cacofonix 66 75 NORP
Asterix and Obelix 26 44 ORG
India 61 66 GPE
Orinjade 122 130 PRODUCT
```

13. Now we will update the small spaCy model and test it on the data:

```
model = "en_core_web_sm"
nlp = train_model(model)
test_model(nlp, DATA)
save_model(nlp, OUTPUT_DIR)
```

The output will be as follows:

```
Losses {'ner': 15.059146494916945}
...
Losses {'ner': 0.007869491956206238}
Cacofonix 0 9 PERSON
Asterix 26 33 PERSON
Obelix 38 44 PERSON
India 61 66 LOC
Orinjade 122 130 PERSON
Asterix 39 46 PERSON
Cacofonix 66 75 PERSON
```

14. The `load_and_test` function will load a model and print its output:

```
def load_and_test(model_dir, data=DATA):
    nlp = load_model(model_dir)
    test_model(nlp, data)
```

15. We can check if the loaded model works the same way:

```
load_and_test(OUTPUT_DIR)
```

The output will be as follows:

```
Asterix 39 46 PERSON
Cacofonix 66 75 PERSON
Cacofonix 0 9 PERSON
Asterix 26 33 PERSON
Obelix 38 44 PERSON
India 61 66 LOC
Orinjade 122 130 PERSON
```

How it works...

In *step 1*, we import the necessary packages and functions. In *step 2*, we define the annotated data list. The list is a list of tuples, where the first element is the sentence being annotated and the second element is a dictionary of entities. The dictionary contains the element where the key is the `entities` string and the value is a list of tuples. Each tuple represents an entity and contains, in order, the start and end characters and the type of the entity.

In *step 3*, we define global variables for the number of iterations the model will be trained for and the directory where it will be saved.

In *step 4*, we define the `save_model` function that takes a model and a directory and saves the model into the directory. If there is no such directory, the function creates it.

In *step 5*, we define the `load_model` function that takes a directory and loads the model that was previously saved there.

The `create_model` function defined in *step 6* either creates a blank English model or loads an existing model. If the `model` parameter passed in is None, then the function creates a blank model, otherwise, it loads the model using the parameter.

In *step 7*, we define the `add_ner_to_model` function, where we add the NER component to the spaCy model pipeline if it's not already present. We return it and the model for further processing.

The `add_labels` function defined in *step 8* adds the labels that the model needs to be trained on to the NER component of the pipeline. The function takes in the annotated data object and reads the labels from the object. Both new and existing labels can be added at this step. For larger quantities of data, it would be better to write a new definition that does not loop through all the data to add the labels. The way the function is defined now, it adds the same label several times.

The `train_model` function from *step 9* prepares the model for training and then trains it. It first creates the model using the `create_model` function defined in *step 6*, then adds the NER component using the `add_ner_to_model` function from *step 7*, and then adds the labels to be trained on using the `add_labels` function. It then disables other pipeline components and begins the training process. It takes the data in batches and updates the model. Finally, it returns the trained model.

In *step 10*, we define the `test_model` function, which prints out the model's labeling for a given text.

In *step 11*, we define the `without_training` function, which shows the output of the spaCy NER labeling without the additional training step. When we run this function in *step 12*, we see that although spaCy can find the entities well, the labels are off. Asterix is labeled as an organization, Cacofonix as a national/religious group, and so on.

In *step 13*, we load the small spaCy model, train it on the two additional sentences, test the model, and save it to the output directory. The tagging of the entities is now correct.

In *step 14*, we define the `load_and_test` function, which loads a saved model and tests it on provided data.

In *step 15*, we load the saved model and test again on the input data and see that it works correctly.

There's more...

Now let's say we would like to create a new entity type, GAULISH_WARRIOR, for all the Gaul warriors mentioned in the Asterix comic series. To do this, we will annotate our data differently and train a new model:

1. Define the NEW_LABEL variable to contain the name GAULISH_WARRIOR and annotate the data with the new label:

```
NEW_LABEL = "GAULISH_WARRIOR"
MODIFIED_DATA = [
    ("A fakir from far-away India travels to Asterix's\
        village and asks Cacofonix to save his land from\
```

```
       drought since his singing can cause rain.",
          {'entities':[(39, 46, NEW_LABEL),
                       (66, 75, NEW_LABEL)]}),
      ("Cacofonix, accompanied by Asterix and Obelix, \
      must travel to India aboard a magic carpet to\
      save the life of the princess Orinjade, who is to\
      be sacrificed to stop the drought.",
          {'entities':[(0, 9, NEW_LABEL),
                       (26, 33, NEW_LABEL),
                       (38, 44, NEW_LABEL),
                       (61, 66, "LOC"),
                       (122, 130, "PERSON")]})
    ]
```

> **Important note**
>
> In this example, we have just two sentences with only a few examples of the new entity. In a real-world setting, you should use a few hundred examples. Also, it is important to include other entities that spaCy recognized before to avoid the problem of *catastrophic forgetting*. See the spaCy documentation for more information: `https://spacy.io/usage/training#example-new-entity-type`.

2. Define a new function for training:

```
def train_model_new_entity_type(model=None):
    random.seed(0)
    nlp = create_model(model)
    (nlp, ner) = add_ner_to_model(nlp)
    ner = add_labels(ner, MODIFIED_DATA)
    if model is None:
        optimizer = nlp.begin_training()
    else:
        optimizer = nlp.resume_training()
    move_names = list(ner.move_names)
    pipe_exceptions = ["ner", "trf_wordpiecer",
                       "trf_tok2vec"]
    other_pipes = [pipe for pipe in nlp.pipe_names if
```

```
                            pipe not in pipe_exceptions]
        with nlp.disable_pipes(*other_pipes), \
        warnings.catch_warnings():
            warnings.filterwarnings("once",
                                    category=UserWarning,
                                    module='spacy')
            sizes = compounding(1.0, 4.0, 1.001)
            for itn in range(N_ITER):
                random.shuffle(MODIFIED_DATA)
                batches = minibatch(MODIFIED_DATA,
                                    size=sizes)
                losses = {}
                for batch in batches:
                    texts, annotations = zip(*batch)
                    nlp.update(texts, annotations,
                               sgd=optimizer, drop=0.35,
                               losses=losses)
                print("Losses", losses)
        return nlp
```

3. Follow the same steps as before to train and test the model:

```
model = "en_core_web_sm"
nlp = train_model_new_entity_type(model)
test_model(nlp, DATA)
```

The output will be as follows:

```
Losses {'ner': 52.82467313932977}
…
Losses {'ner': 42.32477968116291}
Asterix 39 46 GAULISH_WARRIOR
Cacofonix 66 75 GAULISH_WARRIOR
Cacofonix 0 9 GAULISH_WARRIOR
Asterix 26 33 GAULISH_WARRIOR
Obelix 38 44 GAULISH_WARRIOR
India 61 66 LOC
Orinjade 122 130 PERSON
```

See also

The spaCy NER model is a neural network model. You can learn more about its architecture from the spaCy documentation: `https://spacy.io/models#architecture`.

Discovering sentiment analysis

In this recipe, we will use two simple tools for labeling a sentence as having positive or negative sentiment. The first tool is the NLTK Vader sentiment analyzer, and the second one uses the `textblob` package.

Getting ready

We will need the `nltk` and `textblob` packages for this recipe. If you haven't already installed them, install them using these commands:

```
pip install nltk
pip install textblob
```

In addition to this, you will need to run the following from Python the first time you use the Vader sentiment analyzer:

```
>> import nltk
>>nltk.download('vader_lexicon')
```

How to do it...

We will define two functions: one will do sentiment analysis using NLTK, and the other using TextBlob.

Your steps should be formatted like so:

1. Import the packages:

    ```
    from textblob import TextBlob
    from nltk.sentiment.vader import
    SentimentIntensityAnalyzer
    ```

2. Define the `sentences` list:

    ```
    sentences = ["I love going to school!", "I hate going to
    school!"]
    ```

3. Initialize the NLTK sentiment engine:

```
sid = SentimentIntensityAnalyzer()
```

4. Define the `get_blob_sentiment` function, which will use the `textblob` package to determine the sentence sentiment:

```
def get_blob_sentiment(sentence):
    result = TextBlob(sentence).sentiment
    print(sentence, result.polarity)
    return result.polarity
```

5. Define the `get_nltk_sentiment` function, which will use the NLTK `SentimentIntensityAnalyzer`:

```
def get_nltk_sentiment(sentence):
    ss = sid.polarity_scores(sentence)
    print(sentence, ss['compound'])
    return ss['compound']
```

6. First, use the NLTK function on each sentence in the list:

```
for sentence in sentences:
    sentiment = get_nltk_sentiment(sentence)
```

The result will be as follows:

```
I love going to school! 0.6696
I hate going to school! -0.6114
```

7. Now use the TextBlob function:

```
for sentence in sentences:
    sentiment = get_blob_sentiment(sentence)
```

The result will be as follows:

```
I love going to school! 0.625
I hate going to school! -1.0
```

How it works...

In *step 1*, we import the classes that we will need in this recipe. In *step 2*, we define the sentence list that we will use; we include a positive and a negative sentence. In *step 3*, we initialize the NLTK sentiment engine to a global variable, so we don't have to redefine it again every time we need to use it.

In *step 4*, we use the `TextBlob` class to get the sentence sentiment. The class works similarly to spaCy's engine: it takes a sentence and analyzes it for everything at once. The sentiment result is available through the `sentiment` object. The object contains the sentiment score, as well as the subjectivity score. A negative sentiment score means negative sentiment, and a positive sentiment score means positive sentiment. The higher the absolute value of the score, the more confident the system is about it.

In *step 5*, we use the NLTK `SentimentIntensityAnalyzer` object to get the sentiment scores. The `compound` element in the `score` object contains the overall score. Like in the `TextBlob` results, a negative score means negative sentiment and a positive score means positive sentiment, and a higher absolute value means more confidence in the result.

In *step 6*, we print out the results using NLTK, and in *step 7*, using TextBlob. They are very similar. You can test them on your data to see which one performs better for your purposes.

Sentiment for short texts using LSTM: Twitter

In this recipe, we will apply the LSTM algorithm to Twitter data, which we will classify by positive and negative sentiment. This will be similar to the *Using LSTMs for supervised text classification* recipe in the previous chapter. By the end of the recipe, you will be able to load and clean the data, and create and train an LSTM model for sentiment prediction.

Getting ready

For this recipe, we will use the same deep learning packages as before, and an additional package to segment Twitter hashtags, which can be downloaded at `https://github.com/jchook/wordseg`. After downloading, install it using this command:

```
python setup.py install
```

We also need to download the Twitter dataset, which can be found at `https://www.kaggle.com/kazanova/sentiment140`.

We will also use the `tqdm` package to see the progress of functions that take a long time to complete. Install it using the following:

```
pip install tqdm
```

How to do it...

We will load the data, clean it, and then use it to train an LSTM model. We will not use the whole dataset, as it is very large. We will also filter it for language, since it's a multi-language dataset.

Your steps should be formatted like so:

1. Import the necessary functions and packages:

```
import re
import pandas as pd
from tqdm import tqdm
from wordseg import segment
import html
import numpy as np
from sklearn.metrics import classification_report
from sklearn.model_selection import train_test_split
from langdetect import detect
from langdetect.lang_detect_exception import
LangDetectException
from keras.preprocessing.text import Tokenizer
from keras.preprocessing.sequence import pad_sequences
import tensorflow as tf
from keras import Sequential
from tensorflow.keras.layers import Embedding,
SpatialDropout1D, LSTM, Densefrom tensorflow.keras.
callbacks import EarlyStopping
import matplotlib.pyplot as plt
from Chapter04.lstm_classification import plot_model
```

2. Initialize the global variables:

```
MAX_NUM_WORDS = 50000
EMBEDDING_DIM = 500
twitter_csv = \
"Chapter05/training.1600000.processed.noemoticon.csv"
english_twitter = "Chapter05/twitter_english.csv"
```

3. Initialize a tqdm object for use to be able to see the progress of loops:

```
tqdm.pandas()
```

4. The filter_english function takes a pandas DataFrame and filters only English tweets. It also saves the DataFrame to a new, smaller CSV file:

```
def filter_english(df, save_path):
    df['language'] = df['tweet'].progress_apply(
                          lambda t: lang_detect(t))
    df = df[df['language'] == 'en']
    df.to_csv(save_path, encoding="latin1")
    return df
```

5. The get_data function reads the dataset file, gets 160,000 datapoints from it, and filters them for English tweets:

```
def get_data(filename, save_path,
             num_datapoints=80000):
    df = pd.read_csv(filename, encoding="latin1")
    df.columns = ['sentiment', 'id', 'date', 'query',
                  'username', 'tweet']
    df = pd.concat([df.head(num_datapoints),
                    df.tail(num_datapoints)])
    df = filter_english(df, save_path)
    return df
```

6. The `clean_data` function cleans the data by lowercasing all tweets, decoding HTML tags, removing @ mentions and URLs, segmenting hashtags into their component words, removing non-alpha characters, and re-labeling positive tweets with 1 instead of 4:

```python
def clean_data(df):
    #Lowercase all tweets
    df['tweet'] = \
    df['tweet'].progress_apply(lambda t: t.lower())
    #Decode HTML
    df['tweet'] = df['tweet'].progress_apply(
                        lambda t: html.unescape(t))
    #Remove @ mentions
    df['tweet'] = df['tweet'].progress_apply(
                lambda t: re.sub(r'@[A-Za-z0-9]+','',t))
    #Remove URLs
    df['tweet'] = df['tweet'].progress_apply(lambda t:\
                re.sub('https?://[A-Za-z0-9./]+','',t))
    #Segment hashtags
    df['tweet'] = df['tweet'].progress_apply(lambda \
                        t: segment_hashtags(t))
    #Remove remaining non-alpha characters
    df['tweet'] = df['tweet'].progress_apply(lambda \
                    t: re.sub("[^a-zA-Z]", " ", t))
    #Re-label positive tweets with 1 instead of 4
    df['sentiment'] = df['sentiment'].apply(lambda \
                        t: 1 if t==4 else t)
    return df
```

7. The `train_model` function takes a pandas DataFrame and trains, saves, and evaluates the resulting model:

```python
def train_model(df):
    tokenizer = \
    Tokenizer(num_words=MAX_NUM_WORDS,
    filters='!"#$%&()*+,-./:;<=>?@[\]^_`{|}~',
    lower=True)
    tokenizer.fit_on_texts(df['tweet'].values)
```

```
save_tokenizer(tokenizer, 'Chapter05/twitter_tokenizer.
pkl')
    X = \
    tokenizer.texts_to_sequences(df['tweet'].values)
    X = pad_sequences(X)
    Y = df['sentiment'].values
    X_train, X_test, Y_train, Y_test = \
    train_test_split(X,Y, test_size=0.20,
                      random_state=42,
                      stratify=df['sentiment'])
    model = Sequential()
    optimizer = tf.keras.optimizers.Adam(0.00001)
    model.add(Embedding(MAX_NUM_WORDS, EMBEDDING_DIM,
                      input_length=X.shape[1]))
    model.add(SpatialDropout1D(0.2))
    model.add(LSTM(100, dropout=0.5,
              recurrent_dropout=0.5,
              return_sequences=True))

    model.add(LSTM(100, dropout=0.5,
              recurrent_dropout=0.5))
    model.add(Dense(1, activation='sigmoid'))
    loss='binary_crossentropy' #Binary in this case
    model.compile(loss=loss, optimizer=optimizer,
                  metrics=['accuracy'])
    epochs = 15
    batch_size = 32
    es = [EarlyStopping(monitor='val_loss',
                      patience=3, min_delta=0.0001)]
    history = model.fit(X_train, Y_train,
                      epochs=epochs,
                      batch_size=batch_size,
                      validation_split=0.3,
                      callbacks=es)
    accr = model.evaluate(X_test,Y_test)
    print('Test set\n  Loss: {:0.3f}\n  \
```

```
        Accuracy: {:0.3f}'.format(accr[0],accr[1]))
    model.save('Chapter05/twitter_model.h5')
    evaluate(model, X_test, Y_test)
    plot_model(history)
```

8. We will now apply the preceding functions to the data to train the model:

```
df = get_data(twitter_csv)
df = clean_data(df)
train_model(df)
```

The result will look something like this:

```
Epoch 1/25
2602/2602 [==============================] - 1381s 531ms/
step - loss: 0.6785 - accuracy: 0.6006 - val_loss: 0.6442
- val_accuracy: 0.6576
...
Epoch 15/15
2602/2602 [==============================] - 1160s 446ms/
step - loss: 0.4146 - accuracy: 0.8128 - val_loss: 0.4588
- val_accuracy: 0.7861
929/929 [==============================] - 16s 17ms/step
- loss: 0.4586 - accuracy: 0.7861
Test set
  Loss: 0.459
  Accuracy: 0.786
```

	precision	recall	f1-score	support
negative	0.79	0.78	0.79	14949
positive	0.78	0.79	0.79	14778
accuracy			0.79	29727
macro avg	0.79	0.79	0.79	29727
weighted avg	0.79	0.79	0.79	29727

And the loss plot will look something like this:

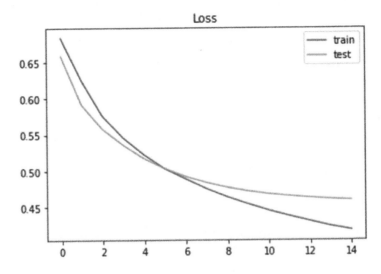

Figure 5.1 – Plot of the loss function for training and test datasets

How it works...

In *step 1*, we import the packages and functions we will use in this recipe. In addition to the already familiar `sklearn` functions, we also import the deep learning functions and classes from `tensorflow`. In *step 2*, we initialize global variables.

In *step 3*, we initialize the `tqdm` object. This object provides progress bars when performing operations on pandas objects.

In *step 4*, we define the `filter_english` function. This function takes a loaded DataFrame and saves only English language tweets. It appends a new column with the tweet language, filters the DataFrame on it, and then saves the filtered DataFrame to the path provided.

In *step 5*, we define the `get_data` function. It loads the full dataset into memory and takes the first and last `num_datapoints` rows, which is 80,000 by default. This is done so that we get an equal amount of positive and negative tweets, as they are sorted by sentiment. We then use the `filter_english` function on the resulting DataFrame and save it to a file.

In *step 6*, we define the `clean_data` function, which does some preprocessing on the English tweets. It first lowercases all tweets, then it removes HTML tags, such as `&amp;`, then it removes the @ mentions and URLs. It then uses the `wordseg` package, which breaks the hashtags into words. Then it removes any remaining non-alphanumeric characters and turns positive sentiment scores into `1` instead of `4`.

In *step 7*, we define the `train_model` function. The function is almost identical to the one we used in the *Using LSTMs for supervised text classification* recipe in the previous chapter, with a few differences. We use a lower learning rate, a different activation function, and a different `loss` function. The difference in the activation and `loss` function, as well as the accuracy metric, is due to the fact that we have only two labels in this case, as opposed to five in the aforementioned recipe. We also increase the depth of the network and increase the dropout rate to avoid overfitting.

In *step 8*, we apply the defined functions to the Twitter data. Using this data, we achieve an accuracy of 79% and the loss function plot still shows some overfitting.

Using BERT for sentiment analysis

In this recipe, we will fine-tune a pretrained **Bidirectional Encoder Representations from Transformers (BERT)** model to classify the Twitter data from the previous recipe. We will load the model, encode the data, and then fine-tune the model with the data. We will then use it on unseen examples.

Getting ready

We will use the Hugging Face transformers library for this recipe. To install the package, run the following command:

```
pip install transformers
```

We will use the same Twitter dataset as in the previous recipe.

How to do it...

BERT models are a little more complicated than the models we were using in previous recipes, but the general idea is the same: *encode the data and train the model*. The one difference is that in this recipe, the model is already pretrained and we will be just fine-tuning it with our data. The steps for this recipe are as follows:

1. Import the necessary functions and packages:

```
import pandas as pd
import tensorflow as tf
import numpy as np
from transformers import BertTokenizer
from transformers import TFBertForSequenceClassification
from tensorflow.keras.layers import Dense
from sklearn.model_selection import train_test_split
from Chapter04.svm_classification import split_dataset
from Chapter04.twitter_sentiment import read_existing_
file, clean_data, plot_model
```

2. Initialize the global variables:

```
batch_size = 32
DATASET_SIZE = 4000
english_twitter = "Chapter04/twitter_english.csv"
tokenizer = \
BertTokenizer.from_pretrained('bert-base-uncased',
                              do_lower_case=True)
max_length = 200
```

3. The `encode_data` function turns the pandas DataFrame into a TensorFlow dataset:

```
def encode_data(df):
    input_ids_list = []
    token_type_ids_list = []
    attention_mask_list = []
    label_list = []
    for index, row in df.iterrows():
        tweet = row['tweet']
```

```
        label = row['sentiment']
        tokenized = tokenizer.tokenize(tweet)
        bert_input = \
        tokenizer.encode_plus(tweet,
                                add_special_tokens = True,
                                max_length = max_length,
                                pad_to_max_length = True,
                                return_attention_mask = \
                                True,
                                )
        input_ids_list.append(bert_input['input_ids'])
        token_type_ids_list.append(bert_input[
                                'token_type_ids'])
        attention_mask_list.append(bert_input[
                                'attention_mask'])
        label_list.append([label])
    return tf.data.Dataset.from_tensor_slices(
        (input_ids_list, attention_mask_list,
        token_type_ids_list,
        label_list)).map(map_inputs_to_dict)
```

4. The helper function used by `encode_data` is `map_inputs_to_dict`:

```
def map_inputs_to_dict(input_ids, attention_masks,
                        token_type_ids, label):
    return {
        "input_ids": input_ids,
        "token_type_ids": token_type_ids,
        "attention_mask": attention_masks,
    }, label
```

5. The `prepare_dataset` function takes the DataFrame and returns a TensorFlow Dataset object:

```
def prepare_dataset(df):
    df = clean_data(df)
    df = pd.concat([df.head(int(DATASET_SIZE/2)),
                    df.tail(int(DATASET_SIZE/2))])
```

```
        df = df.sample(frac = 1)
        ds = encode_data(df)
        return ds
```

6. The `fine_tune_model` function fine-tunes a pretrained BERT model and saves it:

```
def fine_tune_model(ds, export_dir):
    (train_dataset, test_dataset, val_dataset) = \
    get_test_train_val_datasets(ds)
    learning_rate = 2e-5
    number_of_epochs = 3
    model = TFBertForSequenceClassification\
            .from_pretrained('bert-base-uncased')
    optimizer = tf.keras.optimizers.Adam(
                        learning_rate=learning_rate,
                        epsilon=1e-08)
    loss = \
    tf.keras.losses.SparseCategoricalCrossentropy(
                                from_logits=True)
    metric = tf.keras.metrics.\
            SparseCategoricalAccuracy('accuracy')
    model.compile(optimizer=optimizer, loss=loss,
                metrics=[metric])
    bert_history = model.fit(train_dataset,
                    epochs=number_of_epochs,
                    validation_data=val_dataset)
    model.save_pretrained(export_dir)
    return model
```

7. We will now apply the preceding functions to the data to train the model:

```
df = read_existing_file(english_twitter)
dataset = prepare_dataset(df)
model = fine_tune_model(dataset,
                    'Chapter05/bert_twitter_model')
```

Apart from some warnings you can ignore, the result will look something like this:

```
88/88 [==============================] - 4067s 46s/step -
loss: 0.5649 - accuracy: 0.7014 - val_loss: 0.4600 - val_
accuracy: 0.7883
```

8. We can now test our model with new examples using the
    `test_new_example` function:

```
def test_new_example(model_path, tweet):
    model = load_existing_model(model_path)
    bert_input = encode_example(tweet)
    tf_output = \
    model.predict([bert_input['input_ids'],
    bert_input['token_type_ids'],
    bert_input['attention_mask']])[0]
    tf_pred = tf.nn.softmax(tf_output,
                            axis=1).numpy()[0]
    new_label = np.argmax(tf_pred, axis=-1)
    print(new_label)
    return new_label
```

9. Let's use the `test_new_example` function on a new tweet:

```
test_new_example('Chapter04/bert_twitter_test_model',
                 "I hate going to school")
```

The result will be as follows (you can ignore the various warnings):

```
0
```

10. `evaluate_model` loads and evaluates an existing model, and prints out a
    classification report:

```
def evaluate_model(model, X_test, y_test):
    y_pred = []
    for tweet in X_test:
        bert_input = encode_example(tweet)
        tf_output = \
        model.predict([bert_input['input_ids'],
        bert_input['token_type_ids'],
        bert_input['attention_mask']])[0]
```

```
       tf_pred = tf.nn.softmax(tf_output,
                              axis=1).numpy()[0]
       new_label = np.argmax(tf_pred, axis=-1)
       y_pred.append(new_label)
    print(classification_report(y_test, y_pred,
          labels=[0, 1], target_names=['negative',
                                        'positive']))
```

11. The preceding function uses `encode_example`, which takes in text and returns the BERT representation required for the model:

```
def encode_example(input_text):
    tokenized = tokenizer.tokenize(input_text)
    bert_input = \
    tokenizer.encode_plus(input_text,
                          add_special_tokens = True,
                          max_length = max_length,
                          pad_to_max_length = True,
                          return_attention_mask = True,
                          return_tensors='tf'
                          )
    return bert_input
```

12. `load_and_evaluate_existing_model` takes a dataset and an existing fine-tuned model and evaluates it:

```
def load_and_evaluate_existing_model(export_dir):
    model = load_existing_model(export_dir)
    df = read_existing_file(english_twitter)
    df = clean_data(df)
    df = pd.concat([df.head(200),df.tail(200)])
    (X_train, X_test, y_train, y_test) = \
    split_dataset(df, 'tweet', 'sentiment')
    evaluate_model(model, X_test, y_test)
```

13. Apply the `load_and_evaluate_existing_model` function:

```
load_and_evaluate_existing_model(filename)
```

The result will be as follows (you can ignore the various warnings):

	precision	recall	f1-score	support
negative	0.76	0.63	0.69	46
positive	0.60	0.74	0.66	34
accuracy			0.68	80
macro avg	0.68	0.68	0.67	80
weighted avg	0.69	0.68	0.68	80

How it works...

In *step 1*, we import the necessary functions and packages.

In *step 2*, we define global variables. We will use only a small portion of the Twitter dataset, 4,000 datapoints; this is entered in the `DATASET_SIZE` variable. The tokenizer that we use comes from Hugging Face, like the pretrained model, and we load it in the beginning as well. The `max_length` variable specifies how long an input string can be. Since the longest tweet is 178 characters, we set the limit to 200.

In *step 3*, we define the `encode_data` function, which turns text into inputs acceptable to the pretrained BERT model. It uses the `encode_plus` function of the tokenizer. The BERT model doesn't accept just a vector as input as other machine and deep learning models do, but a series of input IDs, token type IDs, and the attention mask.

In *step 4*, we define the `map_inputs_to_dict` function. It maps the inputs and correct labels to a dictionary for a list of inputs.

In *step 5*, we define the `prepare_dataset` function, which takes our Twitter data, cleans it using the `clean_data` function from the previous recipe, encodes it using the tokenizer, and returns a TensorFlow `Dataset` object.

The `fine_tune_model` function defined in *step 6* loads the pretrained model and then trains it further on the data we provide to it, creating a model for further use. The learning rate is much smaller due to the size of the model, and we can use sparse categorical loss and accuracy, since this is a binary output model. In *step 7*, we use the defined functions to train a model. As you can see, with just one epoch of fine-tuning and 20 times less data, we achieve the same accuracy, 78%.

In *step 8*, we define the `test_new_example` function, which uses the trained model to make a prediction for an unseen example. In *step 9*, we use this function on a new tweet, and the result is 0, which indicates a negative sentiment.

In *step 10*, we define a function, `evaluate_model`, which evaluates the model's accuracy and prints out a classification report.

In *step 11*, we define the `encode_example` function, which takes text as input and returns the representation required by the BERT model.

In *step 12*, we define the `load_and_evaluate_existing_model` function. It loads a fine-tuned model, our Twitter dataset, and then calculates the statistics for the model. The data once again needs to be encoded using the BERT tokenizer and turned into tensors, and that is the job of the `encode_example` function, which encodes one example at a time. The accuracy on the test set is lower, which means that it would be good to train the model for more epochs and possibly use more data.

Important note

Fine-tuning BERT models is very computationally intensive. You can try training them in Google Colab or Kaggle.

Testing the model on a new example requires us to encode the text as before, and use the model's `predict` method. After we do that, we need to apply the softmax function to the resulting array, to get the probabilities for each class. Applying the NumPy function `argmax` gets us to the final answer. When we test the model using a new negative sentiment tweet, it indeed returns 0 as the final answer.

There's more...

There are many different pretrained models available, both through Hugging Face and otherwise. For example, Hugging Face provides the `TFDistilBertForSequenceClassification` model, which is more lightweight than the `TFBertForSequenceClassification` model we used in this recipe. There are also other language models and multilingual models that are available.

See also

These are the blog posts I used when researching this recipe: `https://atheros.ai/blog/text-classification-with-transformers-in-tensorflow-2` and `https://towardsdatascience.com/fine-tuning-hugging-face-model-with-custom-dataset-82b8092f5333`.

6
Topic Modeling

In this chapter, we will cover topic modeling, or the unsupervised discovery of topics present in a corpus of text. There are many different algorithms available to do this, and we will cover four of them: **Latent Dirichlet Allocation (LDA)** using two different packages, **non-negative matrix factorization**, K-means with **Bidirectional Encoder Representations from Transformers (BERT)** embeddings, and **Gibbs Sampling Dirichlet Multinomial Mixture (GSDMM)** for topic modeling of short texts, such as sentences or tweets.

The recipe list is as follows:

- LDA topic modeling with sklearn
- LDA topic modeling with gensim
- NMF topic modeling
- K-means topic modeling with BERT
- Topic modeling of short texts

Technical requirements

In this chapter, we will work with the same BBC dataset that we worked with in *Chapter 4, Classifying Texts*. The dataset is available at `https://github.com/PacktPublishing/Python-Natural-Language-Processing-Cookbook/blob/master/Chapter04/bbc-text.csv` in the book's GitHub repository.

LDA topic modeling with sklearn

In this recipe, we will use the **LDA** algorithm to discover topics that appear in the BBC dataset. This algorithm can be thought of as dimensionality reduction, or going from a representation where words are counted (such as how we represent documents using `CountVectorizer` or `TfidfVectorizer`, see *Chapter 3, Representing Text: Capturing Semantics*, we instead represent documents as sets of topics, each topic with a weight. The number of topics is of course much smaller than the number of words in the vocabulary. To learn more about how the LDA algorithm works, see `https://highdemandskills.com/topic-modeling-intuitive/`.

Getting ready

We will use the `sklearn` and `pandas` packages. If you haven't installed them, do so using the following command:

```
pip install sklearn
```

```
pip install pandas
```

How to do it...

We will use a dataframe to parse in the data, then represent the documents using the `CountVectorizer` object, apply the LDA algorithm, and finally print out the topics' most common words. The steps for this recipe are as follows:

1. Perform the necessary imports:

```
import re
import pandas as pd
from sklearn.feature_extraction.text import
CountVectorizer
from sklearn.decomposition import
LatentDirichletAllocation as LDA
from Chapter04.preprocess_bbc_dataset import get_
stopwords
from Chapter04.unsupervised_text_classification import
tokenize_and_stem
```

2. Initialize the global variables:

```
stopwords_file_path = "Chapter01/stopwords.csv"
stopwords = get_stopwords(stopwords_file_path)
bbc_dataset = "Chapter04/bbc-text.csv"
```

3. We then use a function to create the vectorizer:

```
def create_count_vectorizer(documents):
    count_vectorizer = \
    CountVectorizer(stop_words=stopwords,
                    tokenizer=tokenize_and_stem)
    data = count_vectorizer.fit_transform(documents)
    return (count_vectorizer, data)
```

4. The `clean_data` function will remove punctuation and digits:

```
def clean_data(df):
    df['text'] = \
    df['text'].apply(lambda x: re.sub(r'[^\w\s]',
                                      ' ', x))
    df['text'] = \
    df['text'].apply(lambda x: re.sub(r'\d', '', x))
    return df
```

5. The following function will create an LDA model and fit it to the data:

```
def create_and_fit_lda(data, num_topics):
    lda = LDA(n_components=num_topics, n_jobs=-1)
    lda.fit(data)
    return lda
```

6. The `get_most_common_words_for_topics` function will get the most common words for each topic in a dictionary:

```
def get_most_common_words_for_topics(model, vectorizer,
                                     n_top_words):
    words = vectorizer.get_feature_names()
    word_dict = {}
    for topic_index, topic in \
    enumerate(model.components_):
```

```
        this_topic_words = [words[i] for i in \
                topic.argsort()[:-n_top_words - 1:-1]]
        word_dict[topic_index] = this_topic_words
    return word_dict
```

7. The `print_topic_words` function will print the most common words for each topic:

```
def print_topic_words(word_dict):
    for key in word_dict.keys():
        print(f"Topic {key}")
        print("\t", word_dict[key])
```

8. Now we can read the data and clean it. The documents for processing will be in the `text` column of the dataframe:

```
df = pd.read_csv(bbc_dataset)
df = clean_data(df)
documents = df['text']
```

9. We then set the number of topics to 5:

```
number_topics = 5
```

10. We can now create the vectorizer, transform the data, and fit the LDA model:

```
(vectorizer, data) = create_count_vectorizer(documents)
lda = create_and_fit_lda(data, number_topics)
```

11. Now, we create a dictionary with the most common words and print it:

```
topic_words = \
get_most_common_words_for_topics(lda, vectorizer, 10)
print_topic_words(topic_words)
```

The results will vary each time you run it, but one possible output might be as follows:

```
Topic 0
        ['film', 'best', 'award', 'year', 'm', 'star',
        'director', 'actor', 'nomin', 'includ']
Topic 1
        ['govern', 'say', 'elect', 'peopl', 'labour',
```

```
                    'parti', 'minist', 'plan', 'blair', 'tax']
Topic 2
                    ['year', 'bn', 'compani', 'market', 'm', 'firm',
                    'bank', 'price', 'sale', 'share']
Topic 3
                    ['use', 'peopl', 'game', 'music', 'year', 'new',
                    'mobil', 'technolog', 'phone', 'show']
Topic 4
                    ['game', 'year', 'play', 'm', 'win', 'time',
                    'england', 'first', 'player', 'back']
```

How it works...

In *step 1*, we import the necessary packages. We use the `CountVectorizer` object for the vectorizer and the `LatentDirichletAllocation` object for the topic model. In *step 2*, we initialize the path to the stopwords file, and read it into a list, and then initialize the path to the text dataset. In *step 3*, we define the function that creates the count vectorizer and fits it to the data. We then return both the transformed data matrix and the vectorizer itself, which we will use in later steps.

The `clean_data` function in *step 4* removes characters that are not word characters and not spaces (mostly punctuation) as well as digits from the dataset. For this we use the `apply` function on the pandas `Dataframe` object that applies a lambda function that uses the `re` package.

In *step 5*, we define the `create_and_fit_lda` function that creates an LDA model. It takes the vector-transformed data and the number of topics as arguments. The `n_jobs` argument passed in to the LDA object tells it to use all processors for parallel processing. In this case, we know the number of topics in advance, and we can pass that number to the function. In cases where we have unlabeled data, we don't know that number.

In *step 6*, we define the `get_most_common_words_for_topics` function that gets the most frequent words for each topic. It returns a dictionary indexed by the number of the topic.

The `print_topic_words` function in *step 7* will print out the frequent word dictionary.

In *step 8*, we read in the data from the CSV file to a dataframe, remove any unnecessary characters, and then get the documents from the `text` column of the dataframe. In *step 9*, we set the number of topics to 5. In *step 10*, we create the vectorizer and the LDA model.

In *step 11*, we create the most frequent words dictionary and print it. The results correspond well to the predefined topics. Topic 0 relates to entertainment, topic 1 is about politics, topic 2 concerns the economy, topic 3 relates to technology, and topic 4 concerns sports.

There's more...

Let's now save the model and test it on a new example:

1. Import the pickle package:

```
import pickle
```

2. Initialize the model and vectorizer paths:

```
model_path = "Chapter06/lda_sklearn.pkl"
vectorizer_path = "Chapter06/vectorizer.pkl"
```

3. Initialize the new example:

```
new_example = """Manchester United players slumped
to the turf at full-time in Germany on Tuesday in
acknowledgement of what their latest pedestrian first-
half display had cost them. The 3-2 loss at RB Leipzig
means United will not be one of the 16 teams in the draw
for the knockout stages of the Champions League. And
this is not the only price for failure. The damage will
be felt in the accounts, in the dealings they have with
current and potentially future players and in the faith
the fans have placed in manager Ole Gunnar Solskjaer.
With Paul Pogba's agent angling for a move for his
client and ex-United defender Phil Neville speaking of a
"witchhunt" against his former team-mate Solskjaer, BBC
Sport looks at the ramifications and reaction to a big
loss for United."""
```

4. Define the save_model function:

```
def save_model(lda, lda_path, vect, vect_path):
    pickle.dump(lda, open(lda_path, 'wb'))
    pickle.dump(vect, open(vect_path, 'wb'))
```

5. The `test_new_example` function applies the LDA model to the new input:

```
def test_new_example(lda, vect, example):
    vectorized = vect.transform([example])
    topic = lda.transform(vectorized)
    print(topic)
    return topic
```

6. Let's now run the function:

```
test_new_example(lda, vectorizer, new_example)
```

The result will be as follows:

```
[[0.00509135 0.00508041 0.00508084 0.27087506
  0.71387233]]
```

The result is an array of probabilities, one for each topic. The largest probability is for the last topic, which is sport, and the correct identification.

LDA topic modeling with gensim

In the previous section, we saw how to create an LDA model with the `sklearn` package. In this recipe, we will create an LDA model using the `gensim` package.

Getting ready

We will be using the `gensim` package, which can be installed using the following command:

```
pip install gensim
```

How to do it...

We will load the data, clean it, preprocess it in a similar fashion to the previous recipe, and then create the LDA model. The steps for this recipe are as follows:

1. Perform the necessary imports:

```
import re
import pandas as pd
from gensim.models.ldamodel import LdaModel
import gensim.corpora as corpora
```

```
from gensim.utils import simple_preprocess
import matplotlib.pyplot as plt
from pprint import pprint
from Chapter06.lda_topic import stopwords, bbc_dataset,
clean_data
```

2. Define the function that will preprocess the data. It uses the `clean_data` function from the previous recipe:

```
def preprocess(df):
    df = clean_data(df)
    df['text'] = \
    df['text'].apply(lambda x: \
                    simple_preprocess(x, deacc=True))
    df['text'] = \
    df['text'].apply(lambda x: [word for word in x if \
                    word not in stopwords])
    return df
```

3. The `create_lda_model` function creates and returns the model:

```
def create_lda_model(id_dict, corpus, num_topics):
    lda_model = LdaModel(corpus=corpus,
                        id2word=id_dict,
                        num_topics=num_topics,
                        random_state=100,
                        chunksize=100,
                        passes=10)
    return lda_model
```

4. Read and preprocess the BBC dataset:

```
df = pd.read_csv(bbc_dataset)
df = preprocess(df)
```

5. Create the `Dictionary` object and the corpus:

```
texts = df['text'].values
id_dict = corpora.Dictionary(texts)
corpus = [id_dict.doc2bow(text) for text in texts]
```

6. Set the number of topics to be 5 and create the LDA model:

```
number_topics = 5
lda_model = create_lda_model(id_dict, corpus, number_
topics)
```

7. Print the topics:

```
pprint(lda_model.print_topics())
```

The results will vary and may appear as follows:

```
[(0,
  '0.010*"net" + 0.008*"software" + 0.007*"users" +
0.007*"information" + '
  '0.007*"people" + 0.006*"attacks" + 0.006*"computer" +
0.006*"data" + '
  '0.006*"use" + 0.005*"firms"'),
 (1,
  '0.012*"people" + 0.006*"blair" + 0.005*"labour" +
0.005*"new" + '
  '0.005*"mobile" + 0.005*"party" + 0.004*"get" +
0.004*"government" + '
  '0.004*"uk" + 0.004*"election"'),
 (2,
  '0.012*"film" + 0.009*"best" + 0.006*"music" +
0.006*"year" + 0.005*"show" + '
  '0.005*"new" + 0.004*"uk" + 0.004*"awards" +
0.004*"films" + 0.004*"last"'),
 (3,
  '0.008*"game" + 0.006*"england" + 0.006*"first" +
0.006*"time" + '
  '0.006*"year" + 0.005*"players" + 0.005*"win" +
0.005*"world" + 0.005*"back" '
  '+ 0.005*"last"'),
 (4,
```

```
  '0.010*"bn" + 0.010*"year" + 0.007*"sales" +
0.005*"last" + '
  '0.004*"government" + 0.004*"new" + 0.004*"market" +
0.004*"growth" + '
  '0.004*"spending" + 0.004*"economic"')]
```

How it works...

In *step 1*, we import the necessary functions and variables. In *step 2*, we define the function that preprocesses the data. In this function, we use the clean_data function from the previous recipe that removes punctuation and digits from the texts. We then use the gensim simple_preprocess function, which puts the input into lowercase and tokenizes it. We then remove stopwords from the input.

In *step 3*, we create the LDA model. The inputs to the model are as follows: the corpus, or the transformed texts, the Dictionary object, which is analogous to a vectorizer, the number of topics, the random state, which, if set, ensures model reproducibility, chunk size, or the number of documents that are used in each training chunk, and the passes – the number of times the corpus is passed during training. The more passes that are done through the corpus, the better the model will be.

In *step 4*, we define the function that plots log perplexity against the number of topics in the model. This function creates several models, one each for 2 through 9 topics. It then calculates the log perplexity for each and graphs it.

In *step 5*, we read and preprocess the BBC dataset using the imported and predefined functions. In *step 6*, we create id_dict, a Dictionary object that is analogous to a vectorizer, and then use it to map the input texts to *bags of words* according to their mappings in the id_dict object.

In *step 7*, we create the model using five topics, the id dictionary and the corpus. When we print the topics in *step 8*, we see that the topics make sense and correspond roughly as follows: 0 to tech, 1 to politics, 2 to entertainment, 3 to sports, and 4 to business.

There's more...

Now let's save the model and apply it to novel input:

1. Define the new example:

```
new_example = """Manchester United players slumped to the
turf
at full-time in Germany on Tuesday in acknowledgement of
what their
latest pedestrian first-half display had cost them. The
3-2 loss at
RB Leipzig means United will not be one of the 16 teams
in the draw
for the knockout stages of the Champions League. And this
is not the
only price for failure. The damage will be felt in the
accounts, in
the dealings they have with current and potentially
future players
and in the faith the fans have placed in manager Ole
Gunnar Solskjaer.
With Paul Pogba's agent angling for a move for his client
and ex-United
defender Phil Neville speaking of a "witchhunt" against
his former team-mate
Solskjaer, BBC Sport looks at the ramifications and
reaction to a big loss for United."""
```

2. Define the function that will save the model and the `Dictionary` object:

```
def save_model(lda, lda_path, id_dict, dict_path):
    lda.save(lda_path)
    id_dict.save(dict_path)
```

3. The `load_model` function loads the model and the `Dictionary` object:

```
def load_model(lda_path, dict_path):
    lda = LdaModel.load(lda_path)
    id_dict = corpora.Dictionary.load(dict_path)
    return (lda, id_dict)
```

4. The `test_new_example` function preprocesses the input and predicts the topic using the LDA model:

```
def test_new_example(lda, id_dict, input_string):
    input_list = clean_text(input_string)
    bow = id_dict.doc2bow(input_list)
    topics = lda[bow]
    print(topics)
    return topics
```

5. Save our model and `Dictionary` object:

```
save_model(lda_model, model_path, id_dict, dict_path)
```

6. Let's now use the trained model to make a prediction on the new example:

```
test_new_example(lda_model, id_dict, new_example)
```

The result will appear as follows:

```
[(0, 0.023436226), (1, 0.036407135), (3, 0.758486), (4,
0.17845567)]
```

The prediction is a list of tuples, where the first element in each tuple is the number of the topic and the second element is the probability that this text belongs to this particular topic. In this example, we see that the third topic is the most probable, which is sport, and is the correct identification.

NMF topic modeling

In this recipe, we will use another unsupervised topic modeling technique, **NMF**. We will also explore another evaluation technique, topic model coherence. NMF topic modeling is very fast and memory efficient and works best with sparse corpora.

Getting ready

We will continue using the `gensim` package in this recipe.

How to do it...

We will create an NMF topic model and evaluate it using the coherence measure, which measures human topic interpretability. Many of the functions used for NMF models are the same as for LDA models in the gensim package. The steps for this recipe are as follows:

1. Perform the necessary imports:

```
import re
import pandas as pd
from gensim.models.nmf import Nmf
from gensim.models import CoherenceModel
import gensim.corpora as corpora
from gensim.utils import simple_preprocess
import matplotlib.pyplot as plt
from pprint import pprint
from Chapter06.lda_topic_sklearn import stopwords, bbc_
dataset, new_example
from Chapter06.lda_topic_gensim import preprocess, test_
new_example
```

2. The create_nmf_model function creates and returns the model:

```
def create_nmf_model(id_dict, corpus, num_topics):
    nmf_model = Nmf(corpus=corpus,
                    id2word=id_dict,
                    num_topics=num_topics,
                    random_state=100,
                    chunksize=100,
                    passes=50)
    return nmf_model
```

3. The plot_coherence function plots the coherence of the model as a function of the number of topics:

```
def plot_coherence(id_dict, corpus, texts):
    num_topics_range = range(2, 10)
    coherences = []
    for num_topics in num_topics_range:
        nmf_model = create_nmf_model(id_dict, corpus,
```

```
                                        num_topics)
        coherence_model_nmf = \
        CoherenceModel(model=nmf_model, texts=texts,
                        dictionary=id_dict,
                        coherence='c_v')
        coherences.append(
            coherence_model_nmf.get_coherence())
    plt.plot(num_topics_range, coherences,
            color='blue', marker='o', markersize=5)
    plt.title('Coherence as a function of number of \
            topics')
    plt.xlabel('Number of topics')
    plt.ylabel('Coherence')
    plt.grid()
    plt.show()
```

4. Read and preprocess the BBC dataset:

```
df = pd.read_csv(bbc_dataset)
df = preprocess(df)
```

5. Create the `Dictionary` object and the corpus:

```
texts = df['text'].values
id_dict = corpora.Dictionary(texts)
corpus = [id_dict.doc2bow(text) for text in texts]
```

6. Set the number of topics to be 5 and create the NMF model:

```
number_topics = 5
nmf_model = create_nmf_model(id_dict, corpus,
                            number_topics)
```

7. Print the topics:

```
pprint(nmf_model.print_topics())
```

The results will vary and may appear as follows:

```
[(0,
  '0.017*"people" + 0.013*"music" + 0.008*"mobile" +
0.006*"technology" + '
  '0.005*"digital" + 0.005*"phone" + 0.005*"tv" +
0.005*"use" + 0.004*"users" '
  '+ 0.004*"net"'),
 (1,
  '0.017*"labour" + 0.014*"party" + 0.013*"election" +
0.012*"blair" + '
  '0.009*"brown" + 0.008*"government" + 0.008*"people" +
0.007*"minister" + '
  '0.006*"howard" + 0.006*"tax"'),
 (2,
  '0.009*"government" + 0.008*"bn" + 0.007*"new" +
0.006*"year" + '
  '0.004*"company" + 0.003*"uk" + 0.003*"yukos" +
0.003*"last" + 0.003*"state" '
  '+ 0.003*"market"'),
 (3,
  '0.029*"best" + 0.016*"song" + 0.012*"film" +
0.011*"years" + 0.009*"music" '
  '+ 0.009*"last" + 0.009*"awards" + 0.008*"year" +
0.008*"won" + '
  '0.008*"angels"'),
 (4,
  '0.012*"game" + 0.008*"first" + 0.007*"time" +
0.007*"games" + '
  '0.006*"england" + 0.006*"new" + 0.006*"world" +
0.005*"wales" + '
  '0.005*"play" + 0.004*"back"')]
```

8. Now, let's plot model coherence as a function of the number of topics:

```
plot_coherence(id_dict, corpus, texts)
```

Results, again, might vary and may appear as follows:

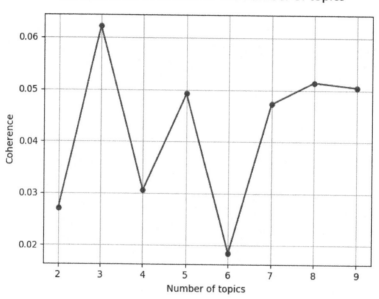

Figure 6.1 – Topic coherence as a function of the number of topics

9. Let's now test a new example, the same example about soccer we used in previous recipes:

```
test_new_example(nmf_model, id_dict, new_example)
```

The result will be as follows:

```
[(2, 0.10007018750350244), (4, 0.8999298124964975)]
```

How it works...

In *step 1*, we import the necessary functions. Many of the functions that work with the `LdaModel` object work the same way with the `Nmf` object.

In *step 2*, we have the `create_nmf_model` function that takes in the corpus of texts, encoded using the `Dictionary` object, the `Dictionary` object itself, the number of topics, the random state that ensures model reproducibility, chunk size, and the number of passes through the corpus.

In *step 3*, we create the `plot_coherence` function that plots the coherence measure against the number of topics in the model. We create a separate NMF model for 2 to 9 topics and measure their coherence.

In *step 4*, we read and preprocess the BBC dataset. In *step 5*, we create the `Dictionary` object and use it to encode the texts creating a corpus. In *step 6*, we set the number of topics to 5 and create the NMF model. In *step 7*, we then print the topics, which look very similar to the ones modeled by the LDA.

In *step 8*, we plot topic coherence. The plot shows the best coherence for 3, 5, and 8 topics. The more topics, the more granular they will be, so it might be the case that 8 topics make sense, and they divide the 5 main topics into coherent subtopics.

In *step 9*, we test the model with a new example about sports, defined in the *LDA topic modeling with genism* recipe, and it shows topic 4 as the most probable, which is sport, and is correct.

K-means topic modeling with BERT

In this recipe, we will use the K-means algorithm to execute unsupervised topic classification, using the BERT embeddings to encode the data. This recipe shares lots of commonalities with the *Clustering sentences using K-means: unsupervised text classification* recipe from *Chapter 4, Classifying Texts*.

Getting ready

We will be using the `sklearn.cluster.KMeans` object to do the unsupervised clustering, along with Hugging Face sentence transformers. To install sentence transformers, use the following commands:

```
conda create -n newenv python=3.6.10 anaconda
conda install pytorch torchvision cudatoolkit=10.2 -c pytorch
pip install transformers
pip install -U sentence-transformers
```

How to do it...

The steps for this recipe are as follows:

1. Perform the necessary imports:

```
import re
import string
import pandas as pd
from sklearn.cluster import KMeans
from nltk.probability import FreqDist
from Chapter01.tokenization import tokenize_nltk
from Chapter04.preprocess_bbc_dataset import get_data
from Chapter04.keyword_classification import divide_data
from Chapter04.preprocess_bbc_dataset import get_
stopwords
from Chapter04.unsupervised_text_classification import
get_most_frequent_words, print_most_common_words_by_
cluster
from Chapter06.lda_topic_sklearn import stopwords, bbc_
dataset, new_example
from Chapter06.lda_topic_gensim import preprocess
from sentence_transformers import SentenceTransformer
```

2. Initialize the global variables and read in the stopwords:

```
bbc_dataset = "Chapter04/bbc-text.csv"
stopwords_file_path = "Chapter01/stopwords.csv"
stopwords = get_stopwords(stopwords_file_path)
```

3. Define the `test_new_example` function:

```
def test_new_example(km, model, example):
    embedded = model.encode([example])
    topic = km.predict(embedded)[0]
    print(topic)
    return topic
```

4. Read in the data and preprocess it:

```
df = pd.read_csv(bbc_dataset)
df = preprocess(df)
df['text'] = df['text'].apply(lambda x: " ".join(x))
documents = df['text'].values
```

5. Read in the sentence transformers model and encode the data using it:

```
model = SentenceTransformer('distilbert-base-nli-mean-tokens')
encoded_data = model.encode(documents)
```

6. Create the `KMeans` model and fit it to the encoded data:

```
km = KMeans(n_clusters=5, random_state=0)
km.fit(encoded_data)
```

7. Print the most common words by cluster:

```
print_most_common_words_by_cluster(documents, km, 5)
```

The result will be as follows:

```
0
['people', 'new', 'mobile', 'technology', 'music',
'users', 'year', 'digital', 'use', 'make', 'get',
'phone', 'net', 'uk', 'games', 'software', 'time', 'tv',
…]
1
['government', 'people', 'labour', 'new', 'election',
'party', 'told', 'blair', 'year', 'minister', 'last',
'bn', 'uk', 'public', 'brown', 'time', 'bbc', 'say',
'plans', 'company', …]
2
```

```
['year', 'bn', 'growth', 'economy', 'sales', 'economic',
'market', 'prices', 'last', 'bank', 'government', 'new',
'rise', 'dollar', 'figures', 'uk', 'rate', 'years', …]
```

```
3
```

```
['film', 'best', 'year', 'music', 'new', 'awards',
'first', 'show', 'top', 'award', 'won', 'number', 'last',
'years', 'uk', 'star', 'director', 'world', 'time',
'band', 'three', …]
```

```
4
```

```
['first', 'year', 'game', 'england', 'win', 'time',
'last', 'world', 'back', 'play', 'new', 'cup', 'team',
'players', 'final', 'wales', 'side', 'ireland', 'good',
'half', 'match', …]
```

8. Now we can test the new sports example using the model:

```
test_new_example(km, model, new_example)
```

The output will be as follows:

```
4
```

How it works...

In *step 1*, we import the necessary packages and functions. We reuse several functions from *Chapter 4*, *Classifying Texts*, and also from previous recipes in this chapter. In *step 2*, we initialize the path to the dataset and get the stopwords.

In *step 3*, we define the test_new_example function, which is very similar to the test_new_example function in previous recipes, the only difference being the encoding of the data. We use the sentence transformers model to encode the data and then the Kmeans model to predict the topic it belongs to.

In *step 4*, we read in the data and preprocess it. The preprocess function tokenizes the text, puts it into lowercase, and removes the stopwords. We then join the word arrays, since the sentence transformers model takes a string as input.

We read in the sentence transformers model and use it to encode the documents in *step 5*. Then, we read in the DistilBERT-based model, which is smaller than the regular model.

In *step 6*, we create the KMeans model, initializing it with five clusters and a random state for model reproducibility.

In *step 7*, we print the most common words by cluster, where cluster 0 is `tech`, cluster 1 is `politics`, cluster 2 is `business`, cluster 3 is `entertainment`, and cluster 4 is `sports`.

In *step 8*, we test the model with a sports example, and it correctly returns cluster 4. Coherence is calculated using Pointwise Mutual Information between each pair of words and then averaging it across all pairs. Pointwise Mutual Information calculates how coincidental it is that two words occur together. Please see more at `https://svn.aksw.org/papers/2015/WSDM_Topic_Evaluation/public.pdf`.

Topic modeling of short texts

In this recipe, we will be using Yelp reviews. These are from the same dataset that we used in *Chapter 3, Representing Text: Capturing Semantics*. We will break the reviews down into sentences and cluster them using the `gsdmm` package. The resulting clusters should be about similar aspects and experience, and while many reviews are about restaurants, there are also other reviews, such as those concerning nail salon ratings.

Getting ready

To install the `gsdmm` package, you will need to create a new folder and then either download the zipped code from GitHub (`https://github.com/rwalk/gsdmm`) or clone it into the created folder using the following command:

```
git clone https://github.com/rwalk/gsdmm.git
```

Then, run the setup script in the folder you installed the package in:

```
python setup.py install
```

How to do it...

In this recipe, we will load the data, divide it into sentences, preprocess it, and then use the `gsdmm` model to cluster the sentences into topics. The steps for this recipe are as follows:

1. Perform the necessary imports:

    ```
    import nltk
    import numpy as np
    import string
    from gsdmm import MovieGroupProcess
    ```

```
from Chapter03.phrases import get_yelp_reviews
from Chapter04.preprocess_bbc_dataset import get_
stopwordss
```

2. Define global variables and load the stopwords:

```
tokenizer = \
nltk.data.load("tokenizers/punkt/english.pickle")
yelp_reviews_file = "Chapter03/yelp-dataset/review.json"
stopwords_file_path = "Chapter06/reviews_stopwords.csv"
stopwords = get_stopwords(stopwords_file_path)
```

3. The `preprocess` function cleans up the text:

```
def preprocess(text):
    sentences = tokenizer.tokenize(text)
    sentences = [nltk.tokenize.word_tokenize(sentence)
                 for sentence in sentences]
    sentences = [list(set(word_list)) for word_list in
                 sentences]
    sentences=[[word for word in word_list if word not
                in stopwords and word not in
                string.punctuation]
               for word_list in sentences]
    return sentences
```

4. The `top_words_by_cluster` function prints out the top words by cluster:

```
def top_words(mgp, top_clusters, num_words):
    for cluster in top_clusters:
        sort_dicts = \
        sorted(mgp.cluster_word_distribution[cluster].\
            items(), key=lambda k: k[1],
            reverse=True)[:num_words]
        print(f'Cluster {cluster}: {sort_dicts}')
```

5. We now read the reviews and preprocess them:

```
reviews = get_yelp_reviews(yelp_reviews_file)
sentences = preprocess(reviews)
```

6. We then calculate the length of the vocabulary that these sentences contain, as this is a necessary input to the GSDMM model:

```
vocab = set(word for sentence in sentences for word in
            sentence)
n_terms = len(vocab)
```

7. Now we can create the model and fit it to the data:

```
mgp = MovieGroupProcess(K=25, alpha=0.1, beta=0.1,
                        n_iters=30)
mgp.fit(sentences, n_terms)
```

8. Now we get the top 15 topics from the model:

```
doc_count = np.array(mgp.cluster_doc_count)
top_clusters = doc_count.argsort()[-15:][::-1]
```

9. We can use the preceding top_words_by_cluster function to print the most important words for each topic:

```
top_words_by_cluster(mgp, top_clusters, 10)
```

Some of the results will appear as follows:

```
Cluster 6: [('chicken', 1136), ('ordered', 1078),
('sauce', 1073), ('cheese', 863), ('salad', 747),
('delicious', 680), ('fries', 539), ('fresh', 522),
('meat', 466), ('flavor', 465)]
Cluster 4: [('order', 688), ('wait', 626), ('table',
526), ('service', 493), ('people', 413), ('asked', 412),
('server', 342), ('told', 339), ('night', 328), ('long',
316)]
Cluster 5: [('menu', 796), ('prices', 400), ('price',
378), ('service', 355), ('selection', 319), ('quality',
301), ('beer', 289), ('delicious', 277), ('options',
274), ('items', 272)]
Cluster 24: [('room', 456), ('area', 425), ('bar',
419), ('people', 319), ('small', 314), ('restaurant',
312), ('clean', 291), ('tables', 283), ('seating', 268),
('inside', 262)]
Cluster 9: [('service', 1259), ('friendly', 1072),
('staff', 967), ('helpful', 317), ('customer', 310),
('attentive', 250), ('experience', 236), ('server', 210),
```

```
('clean', 208), ('people', 166)]
Cluster 3: [('chocolate', 387), ('cream', 339), ('ice',
300), ('tea', 258), ('cake', 219), ('sweet', 212),
('dessert', 186), ('coffee', 176), ('delicious', 176),
('ordered', 175)]
Cluster 18: [('hair', 168), ('nails', 66), ('cut', 60),
('work', 53), ('told', 51), ('massage', 46), ('pain',
46), ('job', 45), ('nail', 43), ('felt', 38)]
...
```

How it works...

In *step 1*, we import the necessary packages and functions. In *step 2*, we define global variables and read in the stopwords. The stopwords used in this recipe are different from other recipes in that they include a number of words that are common to many reviews, such as *good*, *great*, and *nice*. These adjectives and adverbs are very common in reviews, carry no topic information, and the clustering models frequently create topics around them.

In *step 3*, we define the preprocessing function. This function first splits the text into sentences, tokenizes the sentences into words, and removes duplicates from the word lists. The duplicate removal is necessary for the GSDMM model, as it requires a list of unique tokens that occur in the text. The preprocessing function then removes stopwords and punctuation from the word lists.

In *step 4*, we define the top_words_by_cluster function that prints out the most frequent words that appear in each cluster. It sorts the words in each cluster by their frequency and prints out tuples (of word frequency). The number of words per cluster printed is determined by the num_words parameter.

In *step 5*, we read in the reviews and preprocess them using the preprocess function defined in *step 3*.

In *step 6*, we get a set of all the unique words in the review sentences by turning the list of words into a set, and then we assign the count of these words to the n_terms variable to be used later in the creation of the model.

In *step 7*, we create the GSDMM model. The K parameter is the *upper bound* on the number of clusters, as the algorithm determines the number of clusters less than or equal to this number. The `alpha` parameter controls the probability that a new cluster will be created, and the `beta` parameter defines how new text is clustered. If the value of `beta` is closer to 0, then text will be clustered more according to similarity, while if it is closer to 1, the clustering will be more based on the frequency of texts. The `n_iters` parameter determines the number of passes the algorithm makes through the corpus.

In *step 8*, we get the count of documents by topic and then create a list of the 15 most populous topics. We then use this list in *step 9* to get the 10 most frequent words in each cluster.

The results of the clustering make sense for many of the clusters. In the preceding results, cluster 6 is about food, clusters 4 and 9 relate to the service, cluster 5 is about the selection available, cluster 24 concerns the atmosphere, cluster 3 is about dessert, and cluster 18 is about hair and nail salons.

See also

The `gsdmm` package is based on an article by *Yin and Wang, A dirichlet multinomial mixture model-based approach for short text clustering*, which can be found online at `https://www.semanticscholar.org/paper/A-dirichlet-multinomial-mixture-model-based-for-Yin-Wang/d03ca28403da15e75bc3e90c21eab44031257e80?p2df`.

7
Building Chatbots

In this chapter, we will build chatbots using two different frameworks, the `nltk.chat` package and the Rasa framework. The first recipe talks about the `nltk.chat` package, where we build a simple keyword matching chatbot, and the rest of the chapter is devoted to Rasa. **Rasa** is a complex framework that allows the creation of very sophisticated chatbots, and we will have a basic introduction to it. We will build a default bot using Rasa, and then we will modify it to do simple interactions.

Here is the list of this chapter's recipes:

- Building a basic chatbot with keyword matching
- Building a basic Rasa chatbot
- Creating question-answer pairs with Rasa
- Creating and visualizing conversation paths with Rasa
- Creating actions for the Rasa chatbot

Technical requirements

In this chapter, we will use two different packages for our chatbots; one is `nltk.chat` and the other is the Rasa framework. To install these packages, use the following commands:

```
pip install nltk
```

```
pip install rasa
```

Building a basic chatbot with keyword matching

In this recipe, we will build a very basic chatbot that uses keywords to match inquiries and responses. This is based on the `NLTK Chat` class.

Getting ready

We will start by creating a new chat class and initializing it with pairs of responses. Then, we will run it on the command line. If you haven't already, you will need to install the `nltk` package:

```
pip install nltk
```

How to do it...

We will use the NLTK chat framework to create a simple chatbot. First, we will create the question-answer pairs and then create the `Chat` object. We will then use it to converse with the bot:

1. Do the necessary imports:

    ```
    from nltk.chat.util import Chat, reflections
    ```

2. Initialize the conversation pairs:

    ```
    pairs = [[r".*hi|hello|hey|what's up.*",
             ["Hello, I am a simple chatbot. How are you?"]],
            [r'.*(how are you|and you).*',
             ["Doing well, thank you.",
              "I'm ok, what's new?"]],
            [r"quit",
    ```

```
            ["Bye, nice talking to you!",
              "Talk to you later!"]],
            [r".*weather|rain|snow|sun.*",
              ["Isn't it nice out today?",
                "Hopefully, tomorrow the weather will get
                  better.",
                "I don't know about you, but I am glad I am \
                  inside today."]],
            [r"I like (.*)",
              ["Why do you like %1?",
                "What about %1 do you like?"]],
            [r".*(tasty).*", ["Yeah, I think so too."]],
            [r".*",
              ["I am sorry, I don't understand. \
                I am a very simple chatbot!"]]
        ]
```

3. Create a new chatbot:

```
chatbot = Chat(pairs, reflections)
```

4. Use the chatbot's `converse` function to carry out the conversation:

```
chatbot.converse()
```

It might go something like this, where lines preceded by > are user input:

```
>hello
Bot: Hello, I am a simple chatbot. How are you?
>Good, and you?
Bot: I'm ok, what's new?
>I like pizza
Bot: What about pizza do you like?
>It's tasty.
Bot: Yeah, I think so too.
>Do you speak other languages?
Bot: I am sorry, I don't understand. I am a very simple
chatbot!
>quit
Bot: Bye, nice talking to you!
```

How it works...

In *step 1*, we import the `Chat` class and the `reflections` dictionary. This dictionary maps first-person phrases to their corresponding second-person expressions. For example, it will map *I am to you are*.

In *step 2*, we create inquiry-response pairs for the chatbot. The variable is a list of lists. Each sub list has two elements: the first one is the regular expression that we use to match on the user input, and the second one is a list of possible responses, where one is chosen at random. The regular expressions can include groups that can be referenced in the response, as in the `[r"I like (.*)", ["Why do you like %1?", "What about %1 do you like?"]]` list. The `%1` element in the response refers to the `(.*)` group in the input. If you have more than one group, you can refer to them by numbers, as in `%2`, `%3`, and so on. We also include a list with the `.*` input regular expression that has the line `I am sorry, I don't understand. I am a very simple chatbot!` as the response. This regular expression will match anything but only after it tries other expressions, so this is the default option when we don't really know what to say.

In *step 3*, we initialize the chatbot using the reflections dictionary and the inquiry-response pairs. In *step 4*, we use the `converse` function to start the conversation. We see that it matches the inputs that we specified and asks us whether we like pizza. It also uses the default response when it doesn't have an entry for the input `Do you speak other languages?`

There's more...

NLTK has other chatbots that it already created: `eliza_chat`, `iesha_chat`, `rude_chat`, `suntsu_chat`, `zen_chat`. For example, you can try the ELIZA bot as follows:

1. Do the necessary imports:

    ```
    from nltk.chat.eliza import eliza_chat
    ```

2. Initialize the conversation pairs:

    ```
    eliza_chat()
    ```

    The output might look like this:

    ```
    Therapist
    ---------
    Talk to the program by typing in plain English, using normal upper-
    and lower-case letters and punctuation.  Enter "quit" when done.
    ```

```
=========================================================
===============
Bot: Hello.  How are you feeling today?
>Good
Bot: Very interesting.
>I like pizza
Bot: How does that make you feel?
>Hungry
Bot: How does that make you feel?
>quit
Thank you, that will be $150.  Have a good day!
```

Read more about the ELIZA chatbot at `https://en.wikipedia.org/wiki/ELIZA`.

Building a basic Rasa chatbot

In this recipe, we will use a popular chatbot framework, Rasa, to build a default chatbot. In the coming recipes, we will make the chatbot better.

Rasa is an open source deep learning framework for building chatbots. It uses Keras and Tensorflow to implement the model. You can read more about the implementation here: `https://blog.tensorflow.org/2020/12/how-rasa-open-source-gained-layers-of-flexibility-with-tensorflow-2x.html`.

Getting ready

We will initialize the Rasa framework and use it to build and initialize a default Rasa chatbot and then we will explore its structure. If you haven't already, install the rasa package:

```
pip install rasa
```

How to do it...

After installing the `rasa` package, there are new commands available through the Rasa interface. We will use them to create a default chatbot. The steps for this recipe are as follows:

1. On the command line, enter this:

    ```
    rasa init
    ```

    Rasa will start and will produce some colorful output. After that, it will ask you for the path you want to create the new chatbot in. The program output might look like this:

    ```
    2020-12-20 21:01:02.764647: I tensorflow/stream_executor/
    platform/default/dso_loader.cc:48] Successfully opened
    dynamic library cudart64_101.dll

    ┌─────────────────────────────────────────────────────────
    │
    │ Rasa Open Source reports anonymous usage telemetry to
    help improve the product |
    │ for all its users.
    │
    ││
    │ If you'd like to opt-out, you can use `rasa telemetry
    disable`.                 |
    │ To learn more, check out https://rasa.com/docs/rasa/
    telemetry/telemetry.        |
    └─────────────────────────────────────────────────────────

    ...

    Welcome to Rasa! 🤘


    To get started quickly, an initial project will be
    created.

    If you need some help, check out the documentation at
    https://rasa.com/docs/rasa.

    Now let's start! 👇


    ? Please enter a path where the project will be created
    [default: current directory]
    ```

2. Enter the path and press *Enter*:

```
./Chapter07/rasa_bot
```

3. If the path does not exist, Rasa will ask if it needs to be created:

```
? Path './Chapter07/rasa_bot' does not exist 🙂. Create
path?
```

4. Answer `Yes` and then the program will ask you if you want to have an initial model trained:

```
Created project directory at 'C:\Users\zhenya\Documents\
Zhenya\consulting\book\code\python-natural-language-
processing--cookbook\Chapter07\rasa_bot'.
```

```
Finished creating project structure.
```

```
? Do you want to train an initial model? 👍  Yes
```

5. The model will train and Rasa will ask you if you want to interact with the bot; answer `Yes`:

```
? Do you want to speak to the trained assistant on the
command line?    Yes
```

```
2020-12-21 07:20:53 INFO      rasa.model  - Loading model
Chapter07\rasa_bot\models\20201221-071928.tar.gz...
```

```
2020-12-21 07:20:55 INFO      root   - Starting Rasa server
on http://localhost:5005
```

```
2020-12-21 07:20:55 INFO      rasa.model  - Loading model
Chapter07\rasa_bot\models\20201221-071928.tar.gz...
```

```
2020-12-21 07:21:03 INFO      root   - Rasa server is up
and running.
```

```
Bot loaded. Type a message and press enter (use '/stop'
to exit):
```

Our conversation might go something like this:

```
Your input ->  Hello
```
```
Hey! How are you?
```
```
Your input ->  Good, and you?
```
```
Bye
```
```
Your input ->  wow
```
```
Great, carry on!
```
```
Your input ->  where are you located?
```

```
I am a bot, powered by Rasa.
Your input ->  where do you live?
Hey! How are you?
Your input ->  /stop
```

6. Once we input /stop, the program will stop execution and will return to the command line. To power up the chatbot again, change the working directory to the bot path and start it up again:

```
cd Chapter07
cd rasa_bot
rasa shell
```

It will load up again:

```
...

Bot loaded. Type a message and press enter (use '/stop'
to exit):
```

How it works...

In *step 1*, we initialize Rasa. This command is used to create a new chatbot project. In the last line, Rasa asks us about the location of the project files. In *step 2*, we enter a path, an example path is provided, but you can use any path you like. The path specification should follow Unix formatting, so the dot in the path signifies the current directory.

In *step 3*, Rasa asks us if the directory needs to be created. In *step 4*, after we answer Yes, Rasa creates the necessary directories and then asks us if we want to have an initial model trained.

In *step 5*, Rasa asks us if we want to interact with the trained assistant. After we answer Yes, we try out different inputs to see what the bot knows and how it answers. We see that at this point it pretty much recognizes greetings. In the next recipe, we will add some more utterances that it will be able to handle.

In *step 6* we stop the bot. Then we change to the bot directory and power it up again.

There's more...

Let's now look at the file structure of the project:

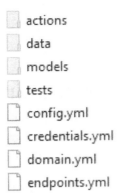

actions
data
models
tests
config.yml
credentials.yml
domain.yml
endpoints.yml

Figure 7.1 – File structure of the project

At the top level, the two most important files are `config.yml` and `domain.yml`. The configuration file specifies how the chatbot should be created and trained, and the `domain.yml` file lists the possible intents it can handle and which responses it should provide for those intents. For example, there is a *greet* intent, and the response to that is `Hey! How are you?` We can modify this file to create our own custom intents and custom responses to those intents.

In addition to the `config.yml` and `domain.yml` files, there are important files in the data directory:

nlu.yml
rules.yml
stories.yml

Figure 7.2 – Files in the data directory

The `nlu.yml` file contains example inputs for each intent. The `rules.yml` file specifies what should be said when. For example, it pairs up the goodbye response with the goodbye intent of the user. Finally, the `stories.yml` file defines conversation paths that might happen during interactions with the user.

See also

Rasa has excellent documentation that can be found at `https://rasa.com/docs/`.

Even this simple bot can be connected to different channels, such as your website, social networks, Slack, Telegram, and so on. See the Rasa documentation on how to do that at`https://rasa.com/docs/rasa/connectors/your-own-website`.

Creating question-answer pairs with Rasa

Now we will build on the simple chatbot that we built in the previous recipe and create new conversation pairs. Our bot will answer simple, frequently asked questions for a business, such as questions about hours, address, and so on.

Getting ready

We will continue using the bot we created in the previous recipe. Please follow the installation instructions specified there.

How to do it...

In order to create new question-answer pairs, we will modify the following files: `domain.yml`, `nlu.yml`, and `rules.yml`. The steps are as follows:

1. Open the `domain.yml` file and in the section named `intents`, add an intent named `hours`. The section should now look like this:

    ```yaml
    intents:
      - greet
      - goodbye
      - affirm
      - deny
      - mood_great
      - mood_unhappy
      - bot_challenge
      - hours
    ```

2. Now we will create a new response for a question about hours. Edit the section named `responses` and add a response named `utter_hours` that has the text `Our hours are Monday to Friday 9 am to 8 pm EST`. The `responses` section should now look like this:

```
responses:
utter_greet:
  - text: "Hey! How are you?"

utter_cheer_up:
  - text: "Here is something to cheer you up:"
    image: "https://i.imgur.com/nGF1K8f.jpg"

utter_did_that_help:
  - text: "Did that help you?"

utter_happy:
  - text: "Great, carry on!"

utter_goodbye:
  - text: "Bye"

utter_iamabot:
  - text: "I am a bot, powered by Rasa."

utter_hours:
  - text: "Our hours are Monday to Friday 9 am to 8 pm
EST."
```

3. Now we will add the user's possible utterances. Open the `nlu.yml` file in the `data` folder and add a section under `nlu` where the intent is `hours` and there are some examples of how the user might inquire about hours. It should look like this (feel free to add more examples):

```
- intent: hours
  examples: |
    - what are your hours?
    - when are you open?
```

```
- are you open right now?
- hours
- open
- are you open today?
- are you open
```

4. We can also use regular expressions to express utterances that contain certain words:

```
- regex: hours
  examples: |
    - \bopen\b
```

5. Now we will add a rule that will make sure that the bot answers about hours when asked about them. Open the `rules.yml` file in the `data` folder and add a new rule:

```
- rule: Say hours when asked about hours
  steps:
  - intent: hours
  - action: utter_hours
```

6. Now we will retrain the model. On the command line, enter the following:

```
rasa train
```

7. We can now test the chatbot. Enter the following on the command line:

```
rasa shell
```

The conversation might go something like this:

```
Bot loaded. Type a message and press enter (use '/stop'
to exit):
Your input ->  hello
Hey! How are you?
Your input ->  what are your hours?
Our hours are Monday to Friday 9 am to 8 pm EST.
Your input ->  thanks, bye
Bye
```

```
Your input -> /stop
2020-12-24 12:43:08 INFO      root  - Killing Sanic server
now.
```

How it works...

In *step 1*, we add an additional intent, hours, and a response that will follow a user's utterance classified as this intent. In *step 2*, we add a response to that intent.

In *step 3*, we add possible ways a user might inquire about hours of operation. In *step 4*, we connect the user's inquiry and the bot's response by adding a rule that ensures that the utter_hours response is given for the hours intent.

In *step 5*, we retrain the model, and in *step 6*, we launch the retrained chatbot. As we see from the conversation, the bot answers correctly to the hours inquiry.

Creating and visualizing conversation paths with Rasa

We will now upgrade our bot to create conversation paths that start and end with greetings and will answer the user's questions about the business' hours and address.

Getting ready

In this recipe, we continue using the chatbot we created in the *Building a basic Rasa chatbot* recipe. Please see that recipe for installation information.

How to do it...

We will add new intents and new replies and create a conversation path that can be visualized. The steps are as follows:

1. We start by editing the domain.yml file. We will first add two intents, address and thanks. The intents section should now look like this:

    ```
    intents:
        - greet
        - goodbye
        - affirm
        - deny
        - mood_great
    ```

```
   - mood_unhappy
   - bot_challenge
   - hours
   - address
   - thanks
```

2. Now we will add three new chatbot utterances to the `responses` section, so it will look like this:

```
responses:
utter_greet:
  - text: "Hey! How are you?"

utter_cheer_up:
  - text: "Here is something to cheer you up:"
    image: "https://i.imgur.com/nGF1K8f.jpg"

utter_did_that_help:
  - text: "Did that help you?"

utter_happy:
  - text: "Great, carry on!"

utter_goodbye:
  - text: "Bye"

utter_iamabot:
  - text: "I am a bot, powered by Rasa."

utter_hours:
  - text: "Our hours are Monday to Friday 9 am to 8 pm
EST."

utter_address:
  - text: "Our address is 123 Elf Road North Pole,
88888."

utter_help:
```

```
    - text: "Is there anything else I can help you with?"


  utter_welcome:
    - text: "You're welcome!"
```

3.   In the `nlu.yml` file in the `data` folder, we will add the possible user utterances for the `address` and `thanks` intents:

```
  - intent: address
    examples: |
      - what is your address?
      - where are you located?
      - how can I find you?
      - where are you?
      - what's your address
      - address

  - intent: thanks
    examples: |
      - thanks!
      - thank you!
      - thank you very much
      - I appreciate it
```

4.   Now we will create stories for possible scenarios. The first scenario will have the user asking about hours and then address, and the other story will have the user first asking about the address and then hours. In the `stories.yml` file, enter the two stories:

```
  - story: hours address 1
    steps:
    - intent: greet
    - action: utter_greet
    - intent: hours
    - action: utter_hours
    - action: utter_help
    - or:
      - intent: thanks
```

```
      - intent: goodbye
    - action: utter_goodbye


  - story: hours address 2
    steps:
    - intent: greet
    - action: utter_greet
    - intent: address
    - action: utter_address
    - action: utter_help
    - intent: hours
    - action: utter_hours
    - intent: thanks
    - action: utter_welcome
    - intent: goodbye
    - action: utter_goodbye
```

5. Now we will train the model and start up the bot:

```
rasa train
rasa shell
```

Our conversation might look like this:

```
Your input ->  hello
Hey! How are you?
Your input ->  what is your address?
Our address is 123 Elf Road North Pole, 88888.
Is there anything else I can help you with?
Your input ->  when are you open?
Our hours are Monday to Friday 9 am to 8 pm EST.
Your input ->  thanks
You're welcome!
Your input ->  bye
Bye
Your input ->  /stop
```

6.   We can visualize all the stories that this bot has. To do that, enter the following command:

```
rasa visualize
```

The program will create the graph and open it in your browser. It will look like this:

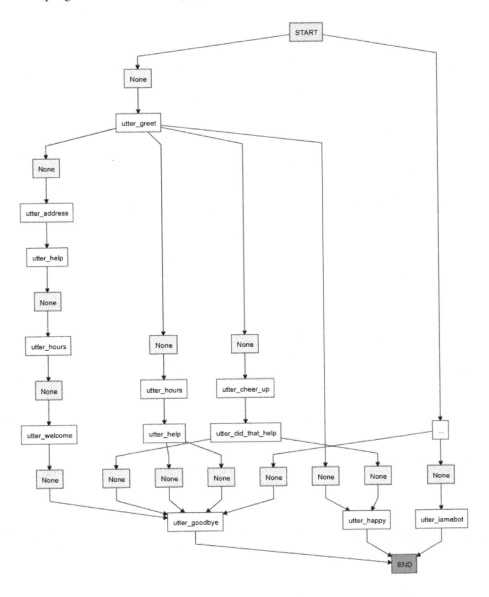

Figure 7.3 – The story graph

How it works...

In *step 1*, we add new intents to the chatbot, and in *step 2*, we add responses to those intents. In *step 3*, we add possible user's utterances for each of the intents added in *step 1*.

In *step 4*, we create possible stories that might come up. In the first story, the user greets the bot and inquires about the hours. After that, one of two intents might come up: either thanks or goodbye, which is handled with an or statement. In the second story, the user first asks about the address and then the hours.

In *step 5*, we train the new model and load the chatbot. The conversation in the example follows the second story.

In *step 6*, we create a visualization graph of all the chatbot stories, including the ones that were predefined. You see that all three stories start with the greeting and continue from there. There is also a rule that is not in any of the stories, and that is answering with the utter_iamabot response to a user's bot_challenge intent.

Creating actions for the Rasa chatbot

In this recipe, we will add a custom action and greet the user by name.

Getting ready

In order to create custom actions, we will need to install the rasa_core_sdk package:

```
pip install rasa_core_sdk
```

How to do it...

We will first edit the configuration files, adding necessary information. Then, we will edit the actions.py file, which programs the necessary actions. We will then start the actions server and test the chatbot:

1. First, in the domain.yml file, add a special intent called inform that may contain entities. The section will now look like this:

```
intents:
  - greet
  - goodbye
  - affirm
  - deny
  - mood_great
```

```
    - mood_unhappy
    - bot_challenge
    - hours
    - address
    - thanks
    - inform
```

2. In the same file, add a new section called `entities` where `name` is the entity:

```
entities:
    - name
```

3. Add a new chatbot utterance that will ask the question about the user's name:

```
responses:
...
utter_welcome:
    - text: "You're welcome!"


utter_ask_name:
    - text: "What's your name?"
```

4. Next, add a section called `actions` in the same file, `domain.yml`, where the one action will be `action_save_name`:

```
actions:
    - action_save_name
```

5. Next, in the `nlu.yml` file, add some examples for the `inform` intent:

```
- intent: inform
  examples: |
    - my name is [Zhenya](name)
    - [Philip](name)
    - [Michelle](name)
    - [Mike](name)
    - I'm [Helen](name)
```

6. In the `stories.yml` file, add the following to each story after the greeting:

```
- action: utter_ask_name
- intent: inform
  entities:
  - name: "name"
- action: action_save_name
```

Our FAQ story will now look like this:

```
- story: hours address 2
  steps:
  - intent: greet
  - action: utter_greet
  - action: utter_ask_name
  - intent: inform
    entities:
    - name: "name"
  - action: action_save_name
  - intent: address
  - action: utter_address
  - action: utter_help
  - intent: hours
  - action: utter_hours
  - intent: thanks
  - action: utter_welcome
  - intent: goodbye
  - action: utter_goodbye
```

7. Now open the `endpoints.yml` file and add or uncomment the following two lines:

```
action_endpoint:
  url: "http://localhost:5055/webhook"
```

8. Now we will edit the `actions.py` file and add our custom action. Open the `actions.py` file, which is located in the `actions` folder of your bot. Add the following code to it:

```python
from typing import Any, Text, Dict, List

from rasa_sdk import Action, Tracker
from rasa_sdk.executor import CollectingDispatcher


class ActionSaveName(Action):

    def name(self) -> Text:
        return "action_save_name"

    def run(self, dispatcher: CollectingDispatcher,
            tracker: Tracker,
            domain: Dict[Text, Any]) -> List[Dict[Text,
                                                  Any]]:
        name = \
        next(tracker.get_latest_entity_values("name"))
        dispatcher.utter_message(text=f"Hello, {name}!")

        return []
```

9. Now open a new terminal, activate the custom environment where Rasa is installed, and run the `actions` endpoint. This will start up the Rasa `actions` server:

```
rasa run actions
```

10. Now train your new model in a terminal window different from the one in *step 8*:

```
rasa train
```

11. Now we can test the bot:

```
rasa shell
```

The conversation might go something like this:

```
Your input ->  hello
```

```
Hey! How are you?
What's your name?
Your input ->Zhenya
Hello, Zhenya!
Your input ->  where are you located?
Our address is 123 Elf Road North Pole, 88888.
Is there anything else I can help you with?
Your input ->  what are your hours?
Our hours are Monday to Friday 9 am to 8 pm EST.
Your input ->  bye
Bye
```

How it works...

In *step 1*, we add the `inform` intent to the list of possible intents. In *step 2*, we add an entity that will be recognized, name. In *step 3*, we add a new utterance that asks about the user's name. In *step 4*, we add a new action that will be triggered when the user answers the question.

In *step 5*, we add sample user inputs for the `inform` intent. You will notice that the names are listed in parentheses and the entity type, name, is listed in square brackets right after the name. The entity name should be the same as the one we listed in *step 2* in the `domain.yml` file.

In *step 6*, we add a piece that asks the user's name and triggers `action_save_name` to each story. The action name should be the same as the one defined in *step 4* in the `domain.yml` file. You will notice that after the `inform` intent, we also list the entities that should be parsed from the user's response, in this case, name.

In *step 7*, we uncomment the lines that tell the Rasa chatbot where to look for the `actions` server, which we will start up in *step 9*.

In *step 8*, we define the `ActionSaveName` class, which defines what should happen when the action is triggered. Each action requires a class that is a subclass of the `Action` class and that overrides two methods, name and run. The name method defines the class name, and that name should be the same as the name we defined in *step 4* in the `domain.yml` file. The run method defines the action that should be taken once the action is triggered. It is given several arguments, including `tracker` and `dispatcher`. The `tracker` object is the chatbot's *memory* and lets us access parsed entities and other information. The `dispatcher` object generates and sends responses back to the user. We get the user's name from the tracker and send the `Hello, {name}!` response.

In *step 9*, we start the `actions` server, which will be accessed during the bot execution. It should be started in a terminal window different from the one where the chatbot is being run.

In *step 10*, we train the bot model, and in *step 11*, we start it up. In the conversation, we now ask the user their name and greet them accordingly.

See also

In addition to parsing entities out, it is possible to parse out information that fills certain slots, for example, departure and destination cities in a bot that provides flight information. This information can be used for lookup and to provide relevant answers to the user. Please see the Rasa documentation for instructions: `https://rasa.com/docs/rasa/forms`.

8

Visualizing Text Data

In this chapter, we will create different types of visualizations. We will visualize the dependency parse, which will show the grammatical relations between words in a sentence. Then, we will visualize different types of verbs in a text using a bar graph. After that, we will look at visualizing named entities in a text. Next, we will create word clouds from a corpus of text, and finally, we will visualize topics created with **Latent Dirichlet Allocation (LDA)** model.

These are the recipes you will find in this chapter:

- Visualizing the dependency parse
- Visualizing parts of speech
- Visualizing NER
- Constructing word clouds
- Visualizing topics

Technical requirements

We will use the following packages in this chapter: spacy, matplotlib, wordcloud, and pyldavis. To install them, use the following commands:

```
pip install spacy
pip install matplotlib
```

```
pip install wordcloud
```

```
pip install pyldavis
```

Visualizing the dependency parse

In this recipe, we will learn how to use the displaCy library and visualize the dependency parse. Details about how to create a dependency parse can be found in *Chapter 2, Getting the Dependency Parse*. We will create two visualizations, one for a short text and another for a long, multi-sentence text.

Getting ready

The displaCy library is part of the spacy package. You need at least version 2.0.12 of the spacy package. If you don't have spacy, install it using the following command:

```
pip install spacy
```

To check the version you have, use the following commands:

```
>>> import spacy
>>> print(spacy.__version__)
2.3.0
>>> exit()
```

If your version is lower than 2.0.12, use the following command to upgrade spacy:

```
pip install -U spacy
```

To validate that the models you have on your computer are compatible with your new version of spacy, use the following command:

```
python -m spacy validate
```

How to do it...

To visualize the dependency parse, we will create the visualize function that will use displacy to show the dependency parse, first of a short text, and then of a long text. We will be able to set different display options:

1. Import the necessary packages:

```
import spacy
from spacy import displacy
from pathlib import Path
```

2. Load the spaCy engine:

```
nlp = spacy.load('en_core_web_sm')
```

3. Define the `visualize` function, which will create the dependency parse visualization:

```
def visualize(doc, is_list=False):
    options = {"add_lemma": True,
               "compact": True,
               "color": "green",
               "collapse_punct": True,
               "arrow_spacing": 20,
               "bg": "#FFFFE6",
               "font": "Times",
               "distance": 120}
    if (is_list):
        displacy.serve(list(doc.sents), style='dep',
                       options=options)
    else:
        displacy.serve(doc, style='dep', options=options)
```

4. Define a short text for processing:

```
short_text = "The great diversity of life today evolved
from less-diverse ancestral organisms over billions of
years."
```

5. Create a `Doc` object and process it using the `visualize` function:

```
doc = nlp(short_text)
visualize(doc)
```

You should see the following output:

```
Using the 'dep' visualizer
Serving on http://0.0.0.0:5000 ...
```

To see the output, load your browser and enter `http://localhost:5000` in the address bar. You should see the following visualization in your browser:

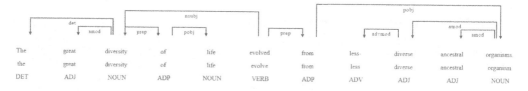

Figure 8.1 – Dependency parse visualization

The visualization server will keep running if you don't explicitly stop it. To stop it, press *Ctrl* + *C* in your Anaconda window.

6.   Now let's define a long text to test the function on:

```
long_text = '''To Sherlock Holmes she is always _the_
woman. I have seldom heard him mention her under any
other name. In his eyes she eclipses and predominates the
whole of her sex. It was not that he felt any emotion
akin to love for Irene Adler. All emotions, and that
one particularly, were abhorrent to his cold, precise
but admirably balanced mind. He was, I take it, the most
perfect reasoning and observing machine that the world
has seen, but as a lover he would have placed himself in
a false position. He never spoke of the softer passions,
save with a gibe and a sneer. They were admirable things
for the observer—excellent for drawing the veil from
men's motives and actions. But for the trained reasoner
to admit such intrusions into his own delicate and finely
adjusted temperament was to introduce a distracting
factor which might throw a doubt upon all his mental
results. Grit in a sensitive instrument, or a crack in
one of his own high-power lenses, would not be more
disturbing than a strong emotion in a nature such as his.
And yet there was but one woman to him, and that woman
was the late Irene Adler, of dubious and questionable
memory.'''
```

7. Run the `visualize` function on the long text:

```
doc = nlp(long_text)
visualize(doc, is_list=True)
```

To see the output, again load your browser and enter `http://localhost:5000` in the address bar. The visualization will list every sentence as a separate tree and the beginning should look like this:

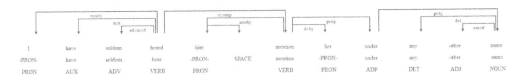

Figure 8.2 – Long text dependency parse visualization

8. Now we will define a function that will save the dependency parse as a `.svg` file:

```
def save_dependency_parse(doc, path):
    output_path = Path(path)
    svg = displacy.render(doc, style="dep",
                          jupyter=False)
    output_path.open("w", encoding="utf-8").write(svg)
```

9. Define the `text` variable and process it using the `spacy` engine again if necessary, and run the preceding function on the `Doc` object:

```
text = "The great diversity of life evolved from less-
diverse ancestral organisms."
doc = nlp(text)
save_dependency_parse(doc, "Chapter08/dependency_parse.
svg")
```

This will create the dependency parse and save it at `Chapter08/dependency_parse.svg`.

How it works...

In *step 1*, we import `spacy` and `displacy`. In *step 2*, we load the spaCy engine.

In *step 3*, we define the `visualize` function. We define different visualization options. The `add_lemma` option adds the word's lemma. For example, the lemma of *evolved* is *evolve* and that is listed under the word itself. The `compact` option pushes the words and arrows together more so it fits in a smaller space. The `color` option changes the color of the words and arrows; for the option values, you can input either color names or color values in hex code. The `collapse_punct` option, if `True`, adds the punctuation to the word before it. The `arrow_spacing` option sets the distance between the arrows in pixels. The `bg` option sets the color of the background, whose value should be either a color name or a color code in hex. The `font` option changes the font of the words. The `distance` option sets the distance between words in pixels. These options are then provided to the `displacy` visualizer as an argument.

For long texts, `displacy` provides an option to show each sentence's parse separately, on a new line. For that, we need to provide the sentences as a list. In the `visualize` function, we use the `is_list` argument. If the argument is equal to `True`, we provide the list of sentences to the `displacy` visualizer; otherwise, we provide the `Doc` object. It is set to `False` by default.

In *step 4*, we define a short text for processing, and in *step 5*, we create the `Doc` object using this sentence and call the `visualize` function. We omit the `is_list` parameter, since this is not a long text. The `displacy.serve` function, when run, starts up the visualization server on `http://localhost:5000` and creates our visualization. When you point your browser to this address, you should see the visualization.

In *step 6*, we define a long text, which is the beginning of *The Adventures of Sherlock Holmes*. In *step 7*, we create a `Doc` object and run the `visualize` function with the `is_list` parameter set to `True`. The visualization is again available at `http://localhost:5000` once the function is run.

You can check out all the visualization options provided by the `displacy` engine at `https://spacy.io/api/top-level#displacy`.

In *step 8*, we define the `save_dependency_parse` function, which saves the parse output at the provided location. It first saves the dependency parse as an object and then writes the resulting object to the path provided.

In *step 9*, we run the preceding function on the short text. Dependency parses for each object should be saved to separate files.

Visualizing parts of speech

As you saw in the *Visualizing the dependency parse* recipe, parts of speech are included in the dependency parse, so in order to see parts of speech for each word in a sentence, it is enough to do that. In this recipe, we will visualize part of speech counts. We will visualize the counts of past and present tense verbs in the book *The Adventures of Sherlock Holmes*.

Getting ready

We will use the `spacy` package for text analysis and the `matplotlib` package to create the graph. If you don't have `matplotlib` installed, install it using the following command:

```
pip install matplotlib
```

How to do it...

We will create a function that will count the number of verbs by tense and plot each on a bar graph:

1. Import the necessary packages:

    ```
    import spacy
    import matplotlib.pyplot as plt
    from Chapter01.dividing_into_sentences import read_text_
    file
    ```

2. Load the `spacy` engine and define the past and present tag sets:

    ```
    nlp = spacy.load("en_core_web_sm")
    past_tags = ["VBD", "VBN"]
    present_tags = ["VBG", "VBP", "VBZ"]
    ```

3. Define the `visualize_verbs` function, which will create the visualization:

```
def visualize_verbs(text_file):
    text = read_text_file(text_file)
    doc = nlp(text)
    verb_dict = {"Inf":0, "Past":0, "Present":0}
    for token in doc:
        if (token.tag_ == "VB"):
            verb_dict["Inf"] = verb_dict["Inf"] + 1
        if (token.tag_ in past_tags):
            verb_dict["Past"] = verb_dict["Past"] + 1
        if (token.tag_ in present_tags):
            verb_dict["Present"] = \
            verb_dict["Present"] + 1
    plt.bar(range(len(verb_dict)),
            list(verb_dict.values()),
            align='center', color=["red","green","blue"])
    plt.xticks(range(len(verb_dict)),
               list(verb_dict.keys()))
    plt.show()
```

4. Run the `visualize_verbs` function on the text of the Sherlock Holmes book:

```
visualize_verbs("Chapter01/sherlock_holmes.txt")
```

This will create the following graph:

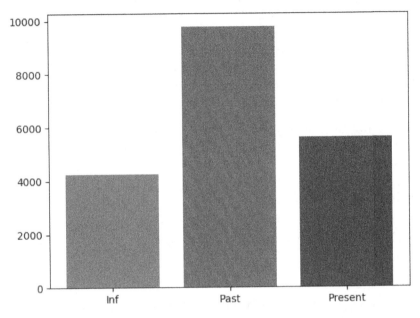

Figure 8.3 – Infinitive, past, and present verbs in The Adventures of Sherlock Holmes

Once the picture is created, you can use the picture controls to save it. After you save it, press *Ctrl + C* at the command prompt to return.

How it works...

In *step 1*, we import the `spacy` package and the `pyplot` interface from `matplotlib`. We also import the `read_text_file` function from the code of *Chapter 1, Learning NLP Basics*, located at `https://github.com/PacktPublishing/Python-Natural-Language-Processing-Cookbook`.

In *step 2*, we create the `spacy` engine and verb tag lists, one for present tense and one for past tense. If you read the *Parts of speech tagging* recipe in *Chapter 1, Overview of NLP*, you will notice that the tags are different from the `spacy` tags used there. These tags are more detailed and use the `tag_` attribute instead of the `pos_` attribute that is used in the simplified tagset.

In *step 3*, we create the `visualize_verbs` function. In this function, we check each token's `tag_` attribute and add the counts of present, past, and infinitive verbs to a dictionary. We then use the `pyplot` interface to plot those counts in a bar graph. We use the `bar` function to define the bar graph. The first argument lists the *x* coordinates of the bars, and the next argument is a list of heights of the bars. We also set the `align` parameter to `center` and provide the colors for the bars using the `color` parameter. The `xticks` function sets the labels for the x axis. Finally, we use the `plot` function to show the resulting plot.

In *step 4*, we run the function on the text of the book *The Adventures of Sherlock Holmes*. The resulting plot shows that most verbs in the book are past tense.

Visualizing NER

To visualize named entities, we will again use `displacy`, the same visualization engine that we used for the visualization of dependency parses.

Getting ready

For this recipe, you will need `spacy`. If you don't have it installed, install it using the following command:

```
pip install spacy
```

How to do it...

We will use `spacy` to parse the sentence and then the `displacy` engine to visualize the named entities. The steps are as follows:

1. Import both `spacy` and `displacy`:

    ```
    import spacy
    from spacy import displacy
    ```

2. Load the `spacy` engine:

    ```
    nlp = spacy.load('en_core_web_sm')
    ```

3. Define the `visualize` function, which will create the dependency parse visualization:

```
def visualize(doc):
    colors = {"ORG":"green", "PERSON":"yellow"}
    options = {"colors": colors}
    displacy.serve(doc, style='ent', options=options)
```

4. Define a text for processing:

```
text = """iPhone 12: Apple makes jump to 5G
Apple has confirmed its iPhone 12 handsets will be its
first to work on faster 5G networks. The company has also
extended the range to include a new "Mini" model that
has a smaller 5.4in screen. The US firm bucked a wider
industry downturn by increasing its handset sales over
the past year. But some experts say the new features
give Apple its best opportunity for growth since 2014,
when it revamped its line-up with the iPhone 6. "5G
will bring a new level of performance for downloads and
uploads, higher quality video streaming, more responsive
gaming, real-time interactivity and so much more," said
chief executive Tim Cook. There has also been a cosmetic
refresh this time round, with the sides of the devices
getting sharper, flatter edges. The higher-end iPhone 12
Pro models also get bigger screens than before and a new
sensor to help with low-light photography. However, for
the first time none of the devices will be bundled with
headphones or a charger."""
```

5. Create a `Doc` object, set its title, and process it using the `visualize` function:

```
doc = nlp(text)
doc.user_data["title"] = "iPhone 12: Apple makes jump to 5G"
visualize(doc)
```

You should see the following output:

```
Using the 'dep' visualizer
Serving on http://0.0.0.0:5000 ...
```

To see the output, load your browser and enter `http://localhost:5000` in the address bar. You should see the following visualization in your browser:

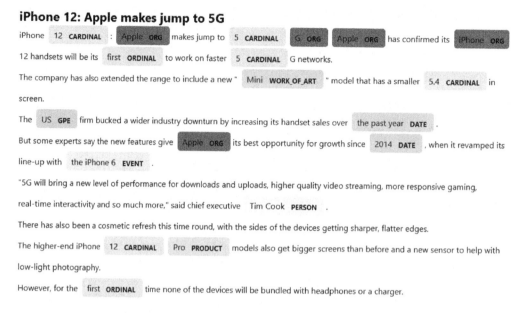

Figure 8.4 – Named entities visualization

6. Now we will define the `save_ent_html` function that will save the visualization as an HTML file:

```
def save_ent_html(doc, path):
    html = displacy.render(doc, style="ent")
    html_file= open(path, "w", encoding="utf-8")
    html_file.write(html)
    html_file.close()
```

7. Use the preceding function on the previously defined `doc` variable:

```
save_ent_html(doc, "Chapter08/ner_vis.html")
```

This will create an HTML file with the entities visualization.

How it works...

In *step 1*, we import the `spacy` and `displacy` packages. In *step 2*, we initialize the `spacy` engine.

In *step 3*, we define the `visualize` function, which will display the visualization. We use custom color settings for the `ORG` and `PERSON` named entities. The color values can be either color names or hex codes.

In *step 4*, we define the text for processing. In *step 5*, we process it using the `spacy` engine. We then set its title to the title of the story; the title will be displayed more prominently in the visualization. We then use the `visualize` function to get the visualization.

In *step 6*, we define the `save_ent_html` function that saves the visualization as `html`. In *step 7*, we use the function to get the `html` file.

Constructing word clouds

In this recipe, we will create two word clouds. Both of them will use the text from the *The Adventures of Sherlock Holmes* book, and one of them will be shaped like a silhouette of Sherlock Holmes' head.

Getting ready

In order to complete this recipe, you will need to install the `wordcloud` package:

```
pip install wordcloud
```

How to do it...

We will define a function to that creates word clouds from text and then use it on the text of *The Adventures of Sherlock Holmes*:

1. Import the necessary packages and functions:

```
import os
import nltk
from os import path
import matplotlib.pyplot as plt
from wordcloud import WordCloud, STOPWORDS
from Chapter01.dividing_into_sentences import read_text_
file
from Chapter01.removing_stopwords import compile_
stopwords_list_frequency
```

2. Define the `create_wordcloud` function:

```python
def create_wordcloud(text, stopwords, filename):
    wordcloud = \
    WordCloud(min_font_size=10, max_font_size=100,
              stopwords=stopwords, width=1000,
              height=1000, max_words=1000,
              background_color="white").generate(text)
    wordcloud.to_file(filename)
    plt.figure()
    plt.imshow(wordcloud, interpolation="bilinear")
    plt.axis("off")
    plt.show()
```

3. Read in the book text:

```python
text_file = "Chapter01/sherlock_holmes.txt"
text = read_text_file(text_file)
```

4. Run the `create_wordcloud` function on the text of the Sherlock Holmes book:

```python
create_wordcloud(text,
                 compile_stopwords_list_frequency(text),
                 "Chapter08/sherlock_wc.png")
```

This will save the result in the file located at `Chapter08/sherlock_wc.png` and create this visualization:

Figure 8.5 – Sherlock Holmes word cloud visualization

How it works...

In *step 1*, we import different packages and functions we will need. We need the `matplotlib.pyplot` and `wordcloud` packages, and in addition, we import the `read_text_file` and `compile_stopwords_list_frequency` functions from *Chapter 1*, *Learning NLP Basics*.

In *step 2*, we define the `create_wordcloud` function. The function takes as arguments the text to be processed, stopwords, and the filename of where to save the result. It creates the `WordCloud` object, saves it to file, and then outputs the resulting plot. The options that we provide to the `WordCloud` object are the minimum font size, the maximum font size, the width and height, the maximum number of words, and the background color.

In *step 3*, we read in the book text. In *step 4*, we use the defined the `create_wordcloud` function to create the word cloud. The stopwords are created using the `compile_stopwords_list_frequency` function, which returns the top 2% of the words in the text as stopwords (see *Chapter 1, Learning NLP Basics*).

There's more...

We can also apply a mask to the word cloud. Here we will apply a Sherlock Holmes silhouette to the word cloud. The steps are as follows:

1. Do the additional imports:

```
import numpy as np
from PIL import Image
```

2. Using the preceding code, modify the `create_wordcloud` function:

```
def create_wordcloud(text, stopwords, filename,
                     apply_mask=None):
    if (apply_mask is not None):
        wordcloud = WordCloud(background_color="white",
                              max_words=2000,
                              mask=apply_mask,
                              stopwords=stopwords,
                              min_font_size=10,
                              max_font_size=100)
        wordcloud.generate(text)
        wordcloud.to_file(filename)
        plt.imshow(wordcloud, interpolation='bilinear')
        plt.axis("off")
        plt.figure()
```

```
            plt.imshow(apply_mask, cmap=plt.cm.gray,
                        interpolation='bilinear')
        plt.axis("off")
        plt.show()
    else:
        wordcloud = WordCloud(min_font_size=10,
                                max_font_size=100,
                                stopwords=stopwords,
                                width=1000,
                                height=1000,
                                max_words=1000,
                                background_color="white")\
                                .generate(text)
        wordcloud.to_file(filename)
        plt.figure()
        plt.imshow(wordcloud, interpolation="bilinear")
        plt.axis("off")
        plt.show()
```

3. Read in the book text:

```
text_file = "Chapter01/sherlock_holmes.txt"
text = read_text_file(text_file)
```

4. Read in the mask and run the function on the text of the Sherlock Holmes book:

```
sherlock_data = Image.open("Chapter08/sherlock.png")
sherlock_mask = np.array(sherlock_data)
create_wordcloud(text,
                compile_stopwords_list_frequency(text),
                "Chapter08/sherlock_mask.png",
                apply_mask=sherlock_mask)
```

This will save the result in the file located at `Chapter08/sherlock_mask.png` and create this visualization:

Figure 8.6 – Word cloud with mask

When creating the result, this program will show two figures: one is the black-and-white image of the silhouette, and the other one is the word cloud with the mask applied.

See also

Please see the `wordcloud` docs, `https://amueller.github.io/word_cloud/`, for more options.

Visualizing topics

In this recipe, we will visualize the LDA topic model that we created in *Chapter 6, Topic Modeling*. The visualization will allow us to quickly see words that are most relevant to a topic and the distances between topics.

> **Important note**
>
> Please see *Chapter 6, Topic Modeling*, for how to create the LDA model that we will visualize here.

Getting ready

We will use the `pyLDAvis` package to create the visualization. To install it, use the following command:

```
pip install pyldavis
```

How to do it...

We will load the model we created in *Chapter 6, Topic Modeling* and then use the `pyLDAvis` package to create the topic model visualization. The visualization is created using a web server:

1. Import the necessary packages and functions:

    ```
    import gensim
    import pyLDAvis.gensim
    ```

2. Load the dictionary, corpus, and LDA model created in *Chapter 6, Topic Modeling*:

    ```
    dictionary = \
    gensim.corpora.Dictionary.load('Chapter06/gensim/id2word.
    dict')
    corpus = gensim.corpora.MmCorpus('Chapter06/gensim/
    corpus.mm')
    lda = \
    gensim.models.ldamodel.LdaModel.load('Chapter06/gensim/
    lda_gensim.model')
    ```

3. Create the `PreparedData` object that will be displayed:

    ```
    lda_prepared = pyLDAvis.gensim.prepare(lda, corpus,
                                          dictionary)
    ```

4. Show the topic model in your browser. Press *Ctrl* + *C* on the command line to stop the server from running:

    ```
    pyLDAvis.show(lda_prepared)
    ```

This will create the following visualization:

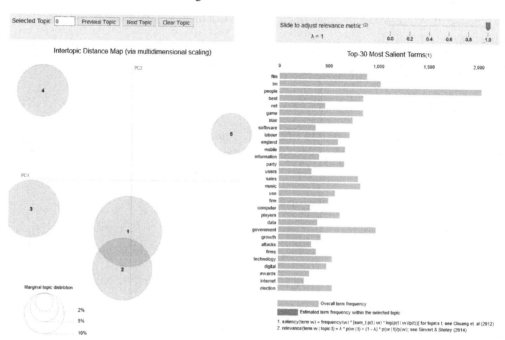

Figure 8.7 – LDA model visualization

5. Save the visualization as `html`:

```
pyLDAvis.save_html(lda_prepared, 'Chapter08/lda.html')
```

How it works...

In *step 1*, we load the `gensim` and `pyLDAvis` packages. In *step 2*, we load the model objects that we created in *Chapter 6, Topic Modeling*, when we created the LDA model: the dictionary, the corpus, and the model itself. In *step 3*, we use `pyLDAvis` to create a `PreparedData` object that we will later render as `html`.

In *step 4*, we show the visualization. This starts up a server and opens the browser to show the visualization. You will see the topics and the words that are important for each topic. To select a particular topic, hover over it with the mouse. Topic 1 is `politics`, topic 2 is `business`, topic 3 is `sports`, topic 4 is `entertainment`, and topic 5 is `tech`. You will see the most important words for each topic change while hovering over them. As expected, politics and business are closely related, even intertwined, and the rest of the topics are separate from each other.

In *step 5*, we save the visualization as `html`.

See also

Using `pyLDAvis`, it is also possible to visualize models created using `sklearn`. See the package documentation for more information: `https://github.com/bmabey/pyLDAvis`.

Packt>

Packt.com

Subscribe to our online digital library for full access to over 7,000 books and videos, as well as industry leading tools to help you plan your personal development and advance your career. For more information, please visit our website.

Why subscribe?

- Spend less time learning and more time coding with practical eBooks and Videos from over 4,000 industry professionals

- Improve your learning with Skill Plans built especially for you

- Get a free eBook or video every month

- Fully searchable for easy access to vital information

- Copy and paste, print, and bookmark content

Did you know that Packt offers eBook versions of every book published, with PDF and ePub files available? You can upgrade to the eBook version at packt.com and as a print book customer, you are entitled to a discount on the eBook copy. Get in touch with us at customercare@packtpub.com for more details.

At www.packt.com, you can also read a collection of free technical articles, sign up for a range of free newsletters, and receive exclusive discounts and offers on Packt books and eBooks.

Other Books You May Enjoy

If you enjoyed this book, you may be interested in these other books by Packt:

Hands-On Python Natural Language Processing

Aman Kedia, Mayank Rasu

ISBN: 978-1-83898-959-0

- Understand how NLP powers modern applications
- Explore key NLP techniques to build your natural language vocabulary
- Transform text data into mathematical data structures and learn how to improve text mining models
- Discover how various neural network architectures work with natural language data
- Get the hang of building sophisticated text processing models using machine learning and deep learning
- Check out state-of-the-art architectures that have revolutionized research in the NLP domain

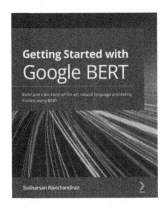

Getting Started with Google Bert

Sudharsan Ravichandiran

ISBN: 978-1-83882-159-3

- Understand the transformer model from the ground up

- Find out how BERT works and pre-train it using masked language model (MLM) and next sentence prediction (NSP) tasks

- Get hands-on with BERT by learning to generate contextual word and sentence embeddings

- Fine-tune BERT for downstream tasks

- Get to grips with ALBERT, RoBERTa, ELECTRA, and SpanBERT models

- Get the hang of the BERT models based on knowledge distillation

- Understand cross-lingual models such as XLM and XLM-R

- Explore Sentence-BERT, VideoBERT, and BART

Packt is searching for authors like you

If you're interested in becoming an author for Packt, please visit `authors.packtpub.com` and apply today. We have worked with thousands of developers and tech professionals, just like you, to help them share their insight with the global tech community. You can make a general application, apply for a specific hot topic that we are recruiting an author for, or submit your own idea.

Leave a review - let other readers know what you think

Please share your thoughts on this book with others by leaving a review on the site that you bought it from. If you purchased the book from Amazon, please leave us an honest review on this book's Amazon page. This is vital so that other potential readers can see and use your unbiased opinion to make purchasing decisions, we can understand what our customers think about our products, and our authors can see your feedback on the title that they have worked with Packt to create. It will only take a few minutes of your time, but is valuable to other potential customers, our authors, and Packt. Thank you!

Index

Made in the USA
Coppell, TX
08 October 2021